Suelyn Medeiros

A MEMOIR

Suelyn Medeiros

iUniverse LLC
Bloomington

SUELYN MEDEIROS
A MEMOIR

iUniverse books may be ordered through booksellers or by contacting:

iUniverse LLC
1663 Liberty Drive
Bloomington, IN 47403
www.iuniverse.com
1-800-Authors (1-800-288-4677)

ISBN: 978-1-4917-2720-1 (sc)
ISBN: 978-1-4917-2721-8 (hc)
ISBN: 978-1-4917-2722-5 (e)

Library of Congress Control Number: 2014903709

Printed in the United States of America.

iUniverse rev. date: 04/03/2014

DEDICATION

This story and book are dedicated to my dear
mother, Elisabete, my father, Sergio, my sisters,
Evelyn and Raquel and the love of my life, Joe.

Above all, my mother taught me how to love
unconditionally and how to forgive.

My father taught me how to be strong, to fight my
battles fairly and to survive no matter what life threw at me.

My sisters made me a better person from the moment
they were born, always pushing me to achieve more and
to do my very best. I hope I set examples for them.

Joe gave me unconditional love and is the best friend I've ever had.
He loves me and supports me in every challenge I'm faced with.
To all my loved ones who played a big part in
who I am today. Thank You. Eu Te Amo.

Acknowledgement

I want to thank God for all He has blessed me with.

I want to give a big thank you to my entire family for their love and support.

I want to thank Joe for being a friend and loving me the way he does. His love and support has inspired me more each day.

I want to thank Robert for helping me throughout this experience to express my stories the best way possible.

Finally, I want to thank my friends and fans for all the love and support you have given me along the way.

Author's Note

Because of a number of unfortunate and recent ugly incidents involving the publishing of memoirs by some writers who intentionally lied and greatly elaborated facts in their stories, it is now common practice for writers and publishers to include an author's note at the beginning of his or her work.

I can tell you what you are about to read is true. However, for various legal reasons, and to protect the innocent, a few names have been changed.

There are also certain passages and descriptions of environments that have been described to the best of my memory and may not be entirely accurate.

If it's a lie to say the trees were barren—and it was winter when it was actually turning to spring—I consider that to be inconsequential to the very real physical and emotional aspects of the story. At its core and heart, my story is uplifting, inspirational, and factual. Keep in mind, it is written in hindsight with all the lessons one learns from trial, error, mistakes, and youth.

An intimate truth is also a universal truth.
—John Cournos

Suelyn Medeiros

PREFACE

The Language of Secrets

@ ^^ # ^^ *&%* (**@~~~@ ##^^^##@9 *)__++
##@^^^%%%6 **^^—) 00 {{{# @@!!.

I F I WERE STILL telling my story secretly, that is how I would
begin.

In my closet today, a large walk-in (some say large enough to
rent out to a small family!) 22 floors above a famous Los Angeles
street that connects the Westside with the East, I have more than 25
journals or diaries—all handwritten using that code, which I prefer
to call my own language.

I didn't create that language overnight, and I didn't develop it for
fun. It came about out of necessity, privacy, and safety. The stories
I carried around in my head and heart from the youngest age were
often not fit for even adult ears—but they are all true—and it is time
to tell them in English, though this will probably be translated into
Portuguese (my second language) as well.

At the earliest age that I was able to comprehend English or
my parents' native tongue, I began to write down my stories in this
manner. At first, they were very simple and weren't even sentences,
but I knew what they meant. I guess I didn't really have to record
my memories at all because they remain with me in every fiber of
my being to this day as vividly as if I'd witnessed a car wreck up
close, firsthand, just this morning. In fact, you could consider some
of my stories just that: tales of horrible car wrecks, metaphorically

speaking. However, don't let that deter you; there are many good ones, too.

My story in its totality is *not* a sad one, no matter how dramatic, heartbreaking, or painful it has been at times. Like just about everyone's life, I've also had plenty to celebrate, much happiness, and good fortune to help temper the nightmares, and I've found that both sides of the life coin are instructional and can lead to a certain peace, if they are approached as lessons.

As I have grown older, I've grown stronger and happier. I still have a long way to travel but I have no regrets and I don't intend to put myself into any situations that would even someday warrant such a thought.

As I got older and understood both English and Portuguese much better, my language became as sophisticated as any other had become, only it was made of hearts, daggers, stars, and shapes—all art in many ways. If I had been born during the 1930s instead of the 1980s, I could have embarrassed the Navajo Code Talkers of World War II.

PART ONE

CHAPTER ONE

A Seven-Year-Old in Queens

O NCE AGAIN, THE MUSIC and laughter are waking me in the middle of the night. I pull the pillow over my head to drown it all out, thinking I can lull myself back to sleep with the pleasant thoughts of my seventh birthday just a week away.

We are living in an old apartment in Queens, New York.

My parents are "playing" again, celebrating nothing in particular with drugs, alcohol, dance, and cards. As the music seems to grow even louder, I can barely hear the clop, clop of their boots and sandals on the worn-out wooden floor down the hall. I throw off the pillow covering my ears. I have to pee. While I shuffle through the kitchen to get to the bathroom, I realize I won't be able to get to sleep for at least another hour. I have on my favorite Barbie pajamas and pull down the bottoms to sit. I'm still a little woozy, keeping my eyes shut, hoping the light won't wake me up too much. Though I close it, of course, I don't lock the door as my parents have taught me in case something happens and they need to get in.

I sit dribbling into the toilet when suddenly the door is thrown open. Instinctively, I clinch my legs together and throw my arms over my lap. It is a tall, burly man who I recognize as one of my father's workers, Marom. He reeks of tequila, sweat, and marijuana. I feel my face flush and quickly say, *"Usando o banheiro,"* Portuguese for, *I'm using the bathroom. I'm almost done.*

I think he's probably drunk and is going to leave, but then he leers at me like a hungry wolf who has stumbled upon a young deer caught in a trap. Immediately, I know I'm in trouble when he extends his arm backwards to close and lock the door with one hand, never turning his eyes away from me. The clack of the bolt feels like a death sentence.

Still, he says nothing, just grinning like an ape as he pulls something out of his pocket, places it up to his nose, and then snorts loudly—a white powder I am more than familiar with; it is the same powder my parents suck up into their noses. Now, I crumple up tightly, my head nearly resting on my lap, and I can feel my heart pounding through my pajama top onto my thighs.

He takes a step toward me and I can see his dirty work boots. My heart is racing so furiously, I think I am going to die.

"I'm finished; can I go?" I ask, actually thinking he might unlock the door. Instead, he takes one final step to me until his knees are touching mine and he is towering over me. *Should I scream for my father?*

My throat is closed and not even a peep escapes my mouth, though I am screeching inside.

"Please," I say, "I want to go." My body is trembling; my legs are pressed together so hard, the blood has stopped flowing into them, and I'm squeezing the fabric of my pajama top so hard, my hands are white.

Suddenly, he grips my chin and pushes my head up.

"I've seen how you look at me," he says, grinning and showing his awful crooked teeth, the color of old corn.

SUELYN MEDEIROS

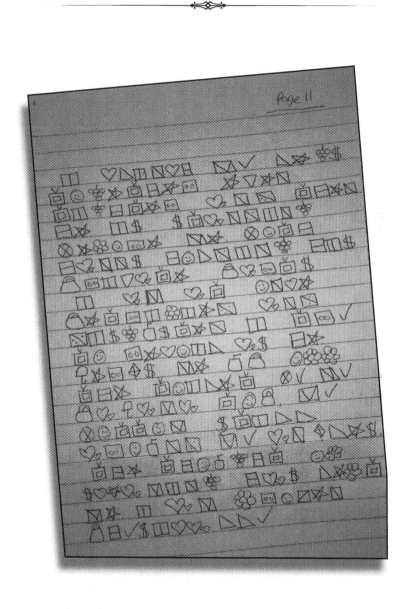

3

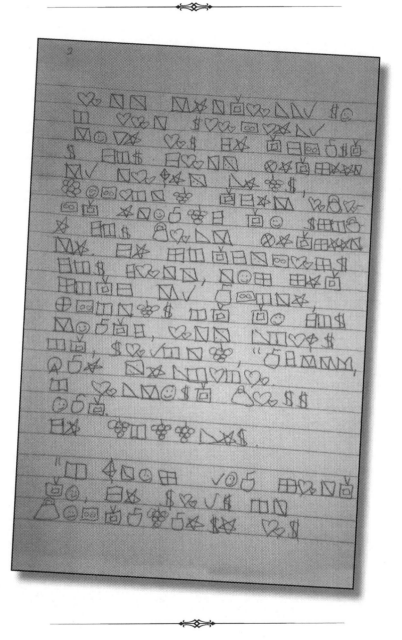

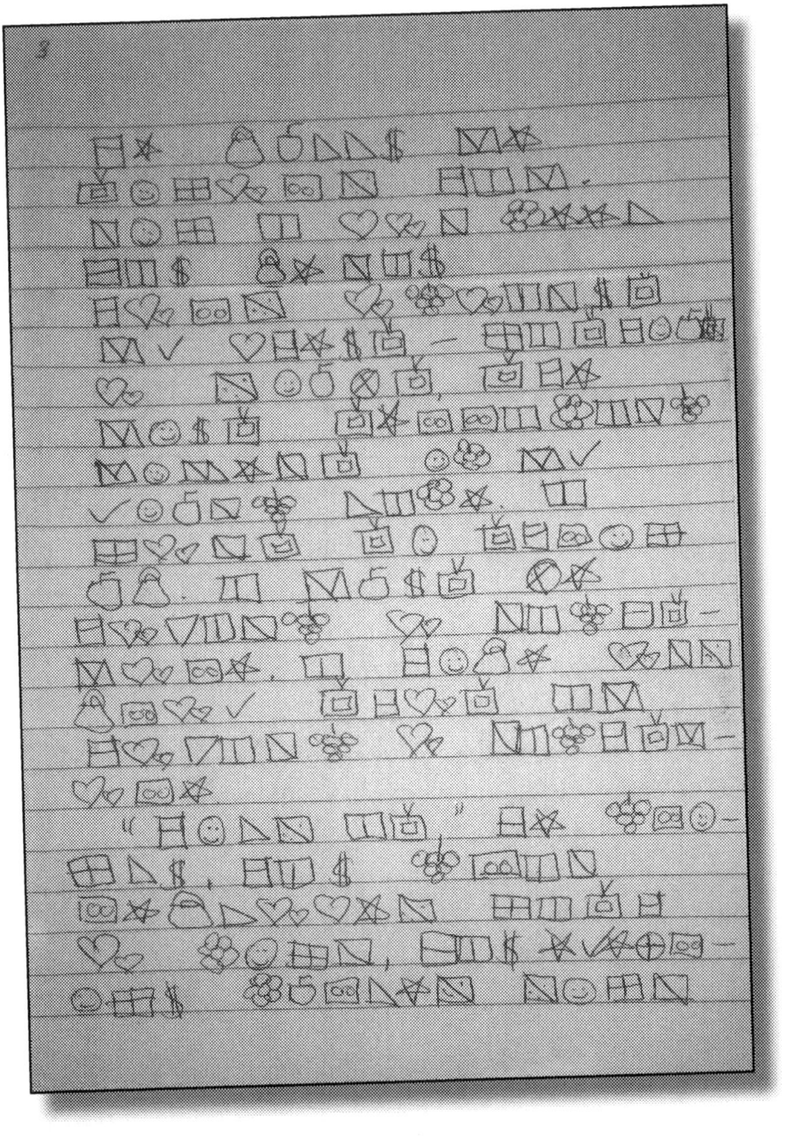

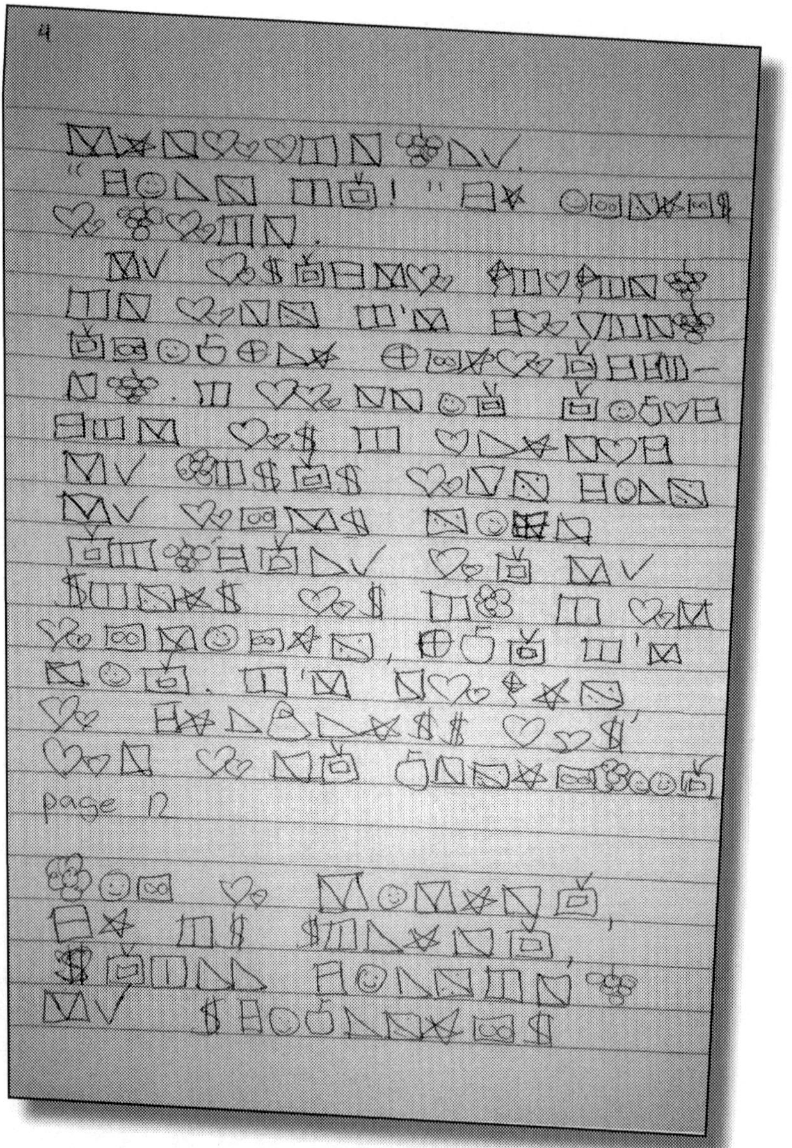
4
page 12

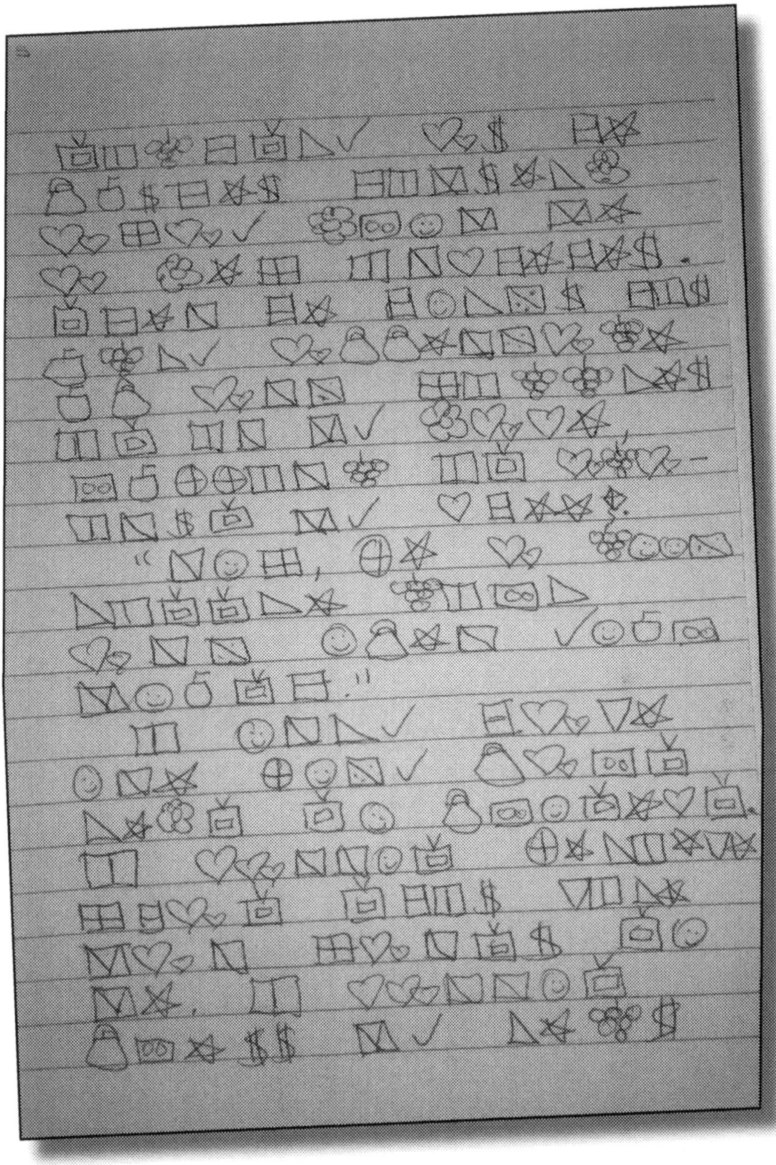

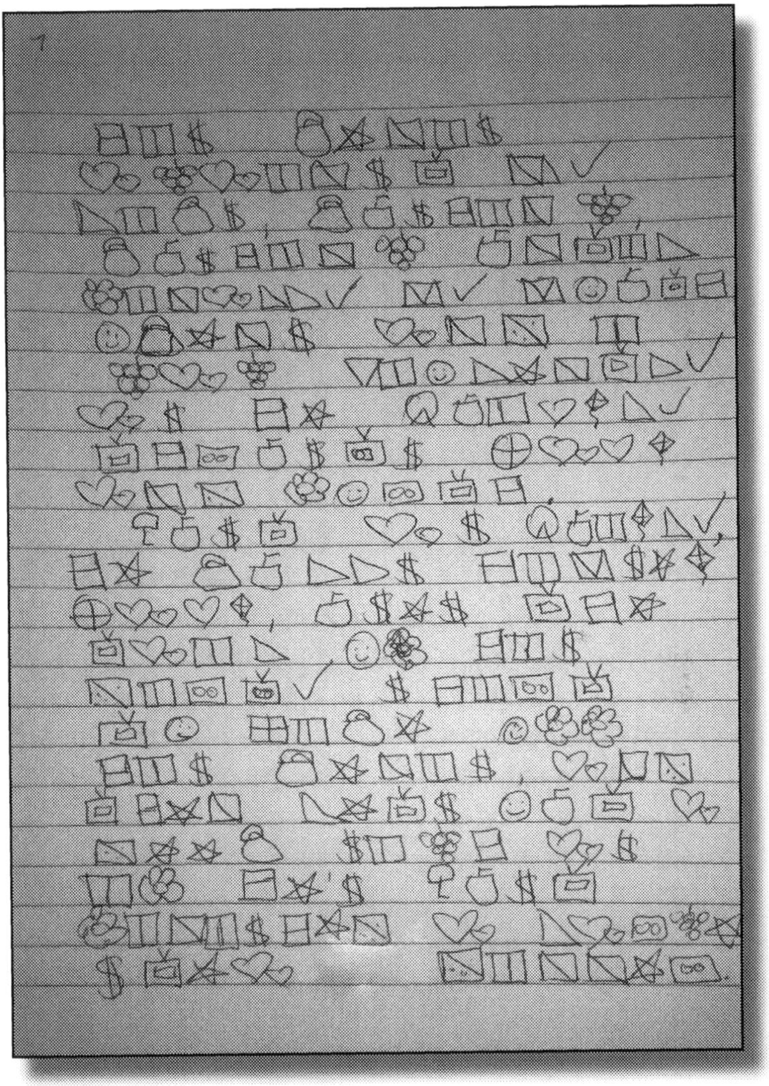

I SLOWLY AND VERY CAREFULLY pull back the bathroom door and peer out into the living room where the party continues. As my eyes trace the faces, I can see my father helping my mother with the white powder. There are about 15 people in the room, arms and feet jerking to the loud music, and then I see him. Our eyes lock. I want to turn away and run, but my feet won't move. He narrows his eyebrows again and moves his lips silently, mouthing in Portuguese, "I will hurt them." Then he crosses his lips with an index finger as if to tell me to be silent.

Now, no one noticing the little girl in the Barbie pajamas, I run down the hall to my room, jump into bed, pull the covers over my head, and lie there awake, trembling and crying until the sun peeks through the window the next morning.

When I sit up, giving up the desire to be asleep, to somehow pretend it was merely a nightmare, I see all my Barbie dolls lined up on the shelf, each of them staring at me with the same expression—*shame on you*, they all say with their eyes—*shame on you!*

Before last night, they were all my friends. I would always play a teacher, or a dancer, or an actor and they would all be my students, partners, or other actors in my movies. Now, they were as disgusted as I was.

In the blink of an eye, my childhood was over.

I stayed in bed waiting for my parents to stir. Usually when they partied, they would sleep late. Today was no exception. I waited. After several hours, my mother came into my room and asked if I was hungry. She wore her ever-present smile and had a lilt in her voice as if this was the best day of our lives—but it wasn't. I lied and told her I'd already had some cereal. She came over and sat on the edge of my bed. She traced the cut on my face around the edges and asked how I'd gotten it. I quickly made up a story about wanting to try to shave as I'd seen Daddy do every morning.

As she stood up, she admonished me not to play with such dangerous things, especially sharp objects. Then she knelt down, hugged me, and in that sweet, sweet soft voice, said, "My little princess. You must be careful. You cannot hurt the most beautiful little face in the world." She kissed the cut, then my forehead. "I love you."

I said, "I love you, too, Mommy."

I WAS BORN IN NEW York. Up until about 10 years ago, I had lived in Queens, New Jersey, Florida, and Brazil (alternately near Rio de Janeiro and practically on the banks of the Amazon River on my grandparents' farm). I now live in Los Angeles, California.

Since I began to model fashions in New York at the age of 19, I've lived all over the world: in Marina del Rey, California, then on and off in Paris, Rio, Mexico, Italy, Amsterdam, London, Germany, the Bahamas, Barbados, and many, many more. Eventually, I considered southern California and Brazil as my primary home bases. However, over the last four years my home has been airports and planes, at least that's the way it feels—a little like George Clooney's character in *Up In The Air*. It's been very busy, but I'm certainly not complaining; it's what I wished for and a far cry from my grandparents' farm.

My parents, Sergio and Elisabete Medeiros, are from Brazil. My father came to America on a student visa, and then months later brought my mother over. Though we moved back and forth several times, I was born on one of their earliest visits to New York in the mid-1980s.

We had tons of family in Brazil; eventually, I had 22 first cousins and I don't know how many second cousins—almost my own town with which to play! My maternal grandparents had 13 children. My mother has 2 brothers and 8 sisters, and they all have children. My cousin, Dayane, who is only a year younger than I am, became my favorite girlfriend. We bonded early and at different points of my life, she became almost as integral a part as my sisters.

My parents could not have been more different and yet, that's one of the effects of their personalities that kept them closely bonded. My father, though he'd driven a cab among other jobs, was essentially a construction worker. He was independent, strong, fun, and always enthusiastic—the more positive of the two, not that my mother was negative, just happily skeptical. She was small at five-feet-four with sweet light brown eyes, light brown hair, and as gentle as a dove—a woman with a beautiful, kind heart. She was also insecure, overly dramatic, and completely dependent upon my father.

My parents had known each other since they were teenagers—maybe been in love that long—and so he was pretty much like a father to her—he handled everything, not to make her dependent, but because he always wanted to protect and take care of her. Seeing how he treated her, I naturally assumed that was every man's motivation for treating women well. I maintained that fantasy until I began to date.

Though they were both close with their parents and were gregarious people who often had friends over, they lived in several worlds, but the constant one was his three girls.

When my father was around, my mother's world was uncomplicated and the future was stable. When he wasn't, she was a basket case: frustrated, weak, and confused.

Since they are the source of my DNA, their strengths and weaknesses run through my veins. Their world was shared and they had us, but although they loved each other completely and unconditionally, they had two very different personalities.

I was always an astute observer of human nature and behavior, even at a very young age; I think the experience I related at the beginning of this chapter, along with others equally as appalling that revolve around men, was the beginning of a lifelong defensive nature: one woman's survival mode, both physically and emotionally.

My parents, being so different and yet so much in love (coupled with my defensive nature), caused me to think about why opposites attract. I've concluded that this phenomenon is a fact of nature. For some reason, it is necessary for the survival of the species, or maybe the survival of everything on earth.

Think about it in physical and mental ways: If you look at a color wheel or have ever taken art classes, you know that "complimentary colors" are the ones that are on the opposite side of the wheel—for example, blue and yellow. When these colors are used adjacent to each other in a painting or in your living room, for that matter, they "compliment" each other, even though they are called "opposites."

Look at the flowers around you; look at everything in nature, and you will see the same laws. When colors are combined that are too "close" to each other on the color wheel or in color theory; they don't work; they don't balance.

Another example is "contrast." Again, in art, it isn't possible to render three-dimensional objects without using contrasts. A ball will appear as just a flat circle if it doesn't have shadows against the light parts. It takes an opposite tone to make it appear as a sphere.

Perhaps the dating sites online already know all this—opposites attract because they create balance.

The examples go on forever. The point is, my parents were very different people and I am nearly the opposite of both of them in many ways; but we all love each other dearly and are very close—we are balanced. My mother was blue, my father was yellow, and I was what you got when you mixed the two—green.

This is my story. It is the story of a close family, lots of love, and a good share of mistakes and disappointments—the same ones we all experience to one extent or another.

No matter how different we all are, we are the same. We are all part of each other and every living thing, which makes life a wild ride!

M Y PARENTS MOVED TO New York in the early 1980s. I was born in 1986, the first of three sisters. My father came to the U.S. with his older brother, Orlando, on a student visa. They came to the "land of opportunity" with a dream to be free and a vision to become rich. They pitched in and bought a taxi, sharing the driving duties. Later, my father got a construction job; he loved to build and was a natural at it.

My First Plane Ride

After my parents settled in America, they would still go to Brazil at least once a year to visit the family. In 1993, at the age of 7, I went with them for the first time. Until then, I was just a New York girl, going to school every day, playing with my friends, living in an upstairs apartment, and often listening to my parents chatter in Portuguese, though they mostly spoke English to me.

The horrific and violent act by my father's worker had just occurred not long before our travels to Rio, and my nightmares were still vivid. It was as if I was repeatedly rewinding the movie of it. I couldn't get away from the visuals or the crime, or my self-imposed silence—I told no one. Maybe that's why it wouldn't disappear.

A certain calm finally came over me when two things happened that summer while we were changing planes in Miami: First, I found a pink diary in the bookstore. It had Strawberry Shortcake on it and an illustration of strawberry designs across the front and back.

For whatever reason, I decided this would be my salvation, not only to relieve myself of some of my burden, but also to express myself—all in secret, of course. I knew I would die if my father ever found the diary and read the story about the crime of his worker in his own home against one of his daughters. He might even kill the man.

I asked my mother to buy the diary and she did.

On the long plane ride to Rio de Janeiro, I sat with my mother, who was busy crocheting a shawl for my grandmother and too occupied to pay attention. I scrunched up against the window, my back turned to my mother. With the small pink pen, I began to make up a code, which was the second thing that happened.

First, I thought about shapes. I created hearts with arrows through them, plain hearts, stars, kites, happy faces, umbrellas, lips, triangles—all simple line drawings that would be quick and easy to use. Then I wrote down the alphabet in a long single line. Under each letter, I assigned a symbol and then laboriously began to write complete words using the thoughts in my mind. I was young and it was a fabulous distraction from the long plane ride.

I practiced so hard, I barely noticed the plane touching down in Rio; but by the time we arrived, I had the beginnings of a code. Later, I would refine it and use a single symbol for an entire word, streamlining it into what would eventually become my own form of shorthand. Oddly enough, as I look back, it seemed that the exercise was also a sort of psychological test. My symbols for a man were not stick figures; they were a happy face and a sad face. My attacker was most definitely a sad face. My father was a happy face. I was already separating out the chaff.

I became so proficient with my code, I wrote an entire book that summer between my playtime and before bedtime. I still have that pink diary, which I hid (along with 24 others of varying colors and materials): some leather, some hardbound books. That first pink one even has a small lock and key, not that it was ever needed.

By the end of that summer, I had pretty much perfected my code. The "real me" wouldn't be exposed. My nightmares, having seen the light of day in writing, would remain safe. The telling of them was the relief valve.

You won't have to imagine what is in them because, ironically, it's now all in this story.

We spent the first week that summer visiting my grandparents, uncles, aunts, and cousins. I'd accumulated two entire journals of notes on all the fun we had and added some stories about my fears and the evil I'd encountered.

When it was time to leave, I was very sad. I'd become close with my cousin, Jackie, and my Aunt Martha, who asked my mother if I could stay with them. Jackie was only two years older than I was, but because I was at least her equal in maturity, we had great fun together.

When a thought occurred to me that I felt was important, I would pull the pink diary out of my backpack and begin writing. I hid the key in my lipstick case and Jackie, seeing me do so, would always ask, "What're you writing?" My pat answer was always the same, "Just all about the fun we had today." Then I would usually snap the book shut and hold it close to my chest. I was forever telling people that my journal was private and that someday I was going to use my notes to write my life story. Jackie laughed about that, as did everyone else I told.

In the end, my stay with Aunt Martha was shorter than expected. Two events while we kids were playing caused a lot of problems and heartache. I am to blame because the ideas were mine.

The first incident was in the aboveground swimming pool. My uncle had purchased a large Dough Boy that summer for the backyard. It was great, but it didn't have a trampoline for jumping and diving as I'd used at the YMCA in New York when taking swimming lessons.

As all the kids were swimming and playing in the pool, I had what I thought was a brilliant idea. There were many worn-out tires stacked in my Uncle Gilson's backyard, probably from the trucks he drove. I envisioned stacking a bunch of them on top of one another to make a diving board, of sorts.

I enlisted my cousin, Junior, who was 10, along with his two friends, to do the stacking alongside the plastic wall of the pool. The three boys stacked all six tires atop one another; but to our dismay, they weren't high enough. I stroked my chin, trying to come up with a solution—and there it was! Across the yard in the weeds was a small discarded table, like a foldout game table.

The four of us carried the table to the pool, set it down, and stacked the tires on top. It was perfect! Since I was very competitive even at 7 (still am), I declared I would be the brave one to go first. I climbed up on the table, which immediately began to wobble on its spindly legs, and then onto the top tire. Everyone was clapping and chanting, "Go, Suelyn, go!"

I straightened my legs, thrust my hands over my head, pointed my fingers, and jumped up and out, over the pool with such energy, that I slid all the way to the other end, breaking the joint where the panels of plastic came together. Suddenly, there was a tsunami of chlorinated water rushing out of the pool onto the yard. Then, one by one all the other panels began to come apart. As the water kept rushing out, the kids kept sliding and being carried away with the rushing water.

It was a mess that made half the yard a mud pit. Junior dropped a dime on me, pointed to me, and said, "Dad, it was Suelyn who did it."

Although I admitted it to my uncle, he still grounded *all* of us for two days.

The other incident involved scary stories; the kids loved them and I loved to tell them, so after we were given a reprieve two days later from being grounded, I took them all into the garage to build a small fire. It was the middle of the day, and I wanted to make it dark. The floor was concrete, so I again enlisted my cousins to gather up firewood, which we then arranged like I'd seen the cowboys do in the movies.

I crumpled up some newspaper into balls, put them under the wood, and lit them. Soon, there was a very small fire—*too* small. So, like I'd seen my uncle do when he wanted to make the fire big for the burgers, I grabbed the bottle of lighter fluid from the grill and gave it to my cousin, telling him to splash a little on the fire. Instead, Junior dropped the bottle, spilling all of the contents onto the fire, which, of course, caused an immediate explosion that nearly burned my eyebrows off.

Kaboom! Everyone began to run in different directions as the fire raced across the concrete, gobbling up a trail of alcohol, and started to climb up the side of my uncle's car!

Needless to say, Uncle Gilson was more than upset. That night, Aunt Martha called my mother and said, "Suelyn's coming home early."

Before my aunt took me to the airport (my uncle wouldn't speak to me), I gave my cousins all my nice clothes. It was my penance. Besides, they couldn't afford such garments and most of them, including my nice shoes, weren't even sold in Brazil.

I'd like to say I was asking for forgiveness or apologizing, but at that age, I wasn't into material things, so my gesture wasn't entirely altruistic—but it did make me feel good to give them away.

When I got home and was putting away my suitcase, my mother came into my room and asked how I'd unpacked everything so quickly.

I said, "I didn't need to unpack. My case was empty."

"What?" she shrieked. "Did your clothes get stolen?"

"No, Momma. I gave them to my cousins."

"Are you crazy? Why did you do that? Those were expensive clothes. We don't have that kind of money to throw away."

"Uh, I felt bad, Momma. They all had raggedy clothes. I wanted them to have something nice for a change because they were so nice to let me stay there," I said, shuffling my feet and bowing my head in mock humility.

I N 1994, ABOUT A year after our Brazil trip, my father got a great job offer in Florida: a very large contract doing 360 homes. Of course, he decided going to Florida for all of us was best. Within weeks, we were on our way.

During this time, I had been begging my mother for a sister (not yet knowing how they were made). I would badger her to get one for me. It didn't matter how she got it, I just wanted a real friend to play with and as it turned out, a month after we arrived in Florida, she told me she was pregnant.

As I recall, she had unfortunately been sick on and off for a long time (but was never correctly diagnosed with Lupus until several years later). We always chalked it up to the flu or exhaustion but now she was pregnant and sick, so we were elated *and* concerned. (I always wondered if my nightly wishes before crawling under the covers had anything to do with my mother's pregnancy.)

Once my mother was pregnant, my parents made many lifestyle changes: For one thing, they stopped drinking and partying. They wanted a new life. Florida seemed like the solution, away from all their friends and bad influences.

I started a new school in Orlando. The area was growing rapidly and the construction industry was booming—a good place for a carpenter and contractor.

My father found a house to rent, a 3-bedroom tract home with a big backyard, a pool, and many yard toys. Almost as soon as we'd moved in, I began to help my mother decorate. My father would leave very early for work and Mom and I would spend the day decorating and making it our home.

Even though it was too soon to know if it would be a girl or a boy, the baby's name was determined almost at conception. I suppose my mother had a premonition. We played with names for months, and then initials, but it finally came down to starting with my mother's first initial and became Evelyn.

We set up Evelyn's room in beautiful whites, yellows, and greens.

We were home when my mother's water broke so we called Dad. I was with her, holding her hand the entire time. Within half an hour, he was at the house rushing us to the hospital. They took her to the labor room immediately.

I wanted to stay by her side, but the nurses said, "No. Please wait over there," pointing to the benches.

I wasn't going to be deterred that easily. I was way past stubborn. My mother asked the doctor, "Please let her come. She's very mature for her age. She wants to be a part of the birth." After having my mother and father sign a release form, the doctor relented.

I was elated; my father was as nervous as a cat in a room full of rocking chairs. He paced, chewed his nails, and then paced more, nonstop. My mother was ready. Her contractions started to increase as she began her breathing exercises. I wanted to see everything, so I didn't leave the doctor's side. The doctor, a woman, explained everything out loud. It seemed an eternity, but then she said, "Okay, there's the head," and sure enough, a bald little head appeared and then slid out like a greasy little glob. My father nearly fainted and I think almost vomited as he left the room. I couldn't get enough. It was the most fascinating thing I'd ever seen or experienced. I didn't even blink because I didn't want to miss a single thing.

"EeeyowwwUeeeee," the baby screamed. I had a little sister! I was beside myself with excitement! The doctor laid the baby next to my mother. A long, very ugly cord dripping with slime came out of my mother and ran up into my sister's belly. I was stunned by the "alien" appearance when the doctor turned to me and said, "Here, Suelyn. You cut the cord."

Huh? What?

"It doesn't look like your father will be able to."

"No. It will hurt. There will be blood," I responded, backing up slightly.

"No. No, there won't be any pain and very little blood. I promise. Here," she said, handing me a pair of scissors, and held my hands to guide me—and I did it: *I cut the cord!* Now, *I* was about ready to pass out! They then handed Evelyn, swathed in soft warm blankets, to my mother, who looked down at her with an expression on her face I'd never seen before.

"Welcome into the world, Evelyn," she said, stroking my sister's forehead.

Yahoo!

However, a few months later the excitement and jubilation soon subsided, replaced by sadness and apprehension because when Evelyn was 8 months old, my father was arrested for immigration violation. We were all stunned, and no one could tell us how long he would be held or where.

Suddenly, my mother was lost and alone. In one of her phone conversations with my father, which were limited to two minutes a week, they decided it was best my mother, Evelyn, and me to go to Brazil and wait for my father there. The plan was, when he was released, he would sell everything in New York and join us in Florida and then in Brazil, my mother could get help from our grandparents.

Therefore, we packed up and went to Brazil. At first, we stayed with Ercy, my paternal grandmother, but my mother didn't get along with her. She wanted to be with people she loved and loved her—her family—so we left Rio de Janeiro on a journey to a strange new place, Rondonia, an area near the Amazon River where my mother's parents, Lucas and Maria, lived.

Rondonia is immense, comprised mostly of jungle and farms. Before we got there, though, we all had to get immunized. One of the shots made my arm swell up like a softball, and I had a fever for three days. Lord knew what kinds of bugs and diseases we would find in the heart of the Amazon jungle, so they just gave us all kinds of shots.

They have no airports in, or even remotely close to Rondonia, so we had to travel by bus, which was a very old, rickety vehicle. I will never forget the time we spent bouncing around on old dirt roads, clinging to the sides of cliffs on roads so narrow they truly looked like a bicycle couldn't fit on them.

The weather, as it always was if it wasn't pouring rain, was unbearably hot. You could cut the humidity with a knife—a very dull knife.

The area where my grandparents' farm was located was so remote, it took us three days and two nights to get there. We must've made at least a hundred stops along the way to either drop someone off or pick someone up in the middle of nowhere.

The bus would spit and choke out black smoke, and we could hear the brakes scraping and squealing as we rumbled to a halt in the middle of the very dense jungle where there were no signs of life. Then, there would suddenly be a woman with two children and several boxes of things standing on the side of the road, which required that the driver secure the brake, get out, climb up to the roof, and tie down their belongings with twine and then usher them aboard the bus. We had two huge suitcases and several smaller ones of our own tied up there.

When we finally arrived in Rondonia, I was amazed at how large my grandparents' farm was—not the house, just the land and orchards.

While we unloaded our belongings, my first thoughts were: *Where do they shop? How do they buy their food and their other supplies?* The answer, I soon found out, was that they didn't. They grew everything they needed right there. They never had to buy anything. I was amazed that people were so self-sustaining. This was an incredibly new world to me! They pumped their own pristine water from a well; made their own soap; and grew rice, beans, corn, and just about any other vegetable and fruit imaginable.

The house wasn't out near the road where the bus dropped us. It was half a mile away, back into the woods, where my grandfather met us with a horse-drawn wagon, which he then helped us load with our considerable amount of luggage.

When we arrived at the house, my first impression was: *How are we all going to live in that?* His property was about 10 acres, but the house was only about 900 square feet. Once we were inside, I realized there were no rooms, no walls, just an "area," which wasn't very big.

The little house had to accommodate my grandmother and grandfather; my mother, sister, and me; and my mother's youngest sister, my Aunt Deborah; six people.

Blankets hung from rope lines to separate the sleeping areas, and there was a kitchen area, if you could call it that. They had no running water and no plumbing—meaning, no sink and no toilet.

I was stunned. I didn't know where to begin in my mind. It was 10 o'clock at night, still about 90 degrees outside, and the bugs were as thick as throwing a handful of rice up into the air with mosquitos the size of raisins.

I was not happy. My mother and sister were not happy, but my grandparents were delirious to have us and just happy about life in general. Now that we had arrived, with the exception of some breathing room, they had everything they needed.

I couldn't sleep that night. I was deeply depressed, thinking I'd fallen off the edge of the earth into some strange land, never to be seen again.

I loved my grandparents. They were so vibrant, happy, and in love. They had everything they ever dreamed of right in front of them. Even if their house was little (but more than a shack), they loved it; it worked for them.

The next morning, a very loud rooster wakened me. He would announce the sun every day afterward. At first, it was annoying but then after a few mornings, I realized it was his song, his job. He was telling the world to wake up and get to work, just as he was doing.

My grandparents had their regular routines, and it didn't bother them at all that there were all these bodies milling about their home. They loved new company. Just after sunrise, my grandfather went out first thing to begin his farming chores while my grandmother sat in a rickety old rocking chair knitting beautiful comforters she was either selling or giving to distant neighbors she often visited on foot.

My grandparents seemed to walk everywhere, which is probably why they were so healthy for their ages—no cars, they didn't use horses although they had them. They were just content to walk and loved doing so.

Grandmother did the house chores: washing dishes, mopping the always-dusty floors, and washing clothes. Since they had no running water, she went outside where the stove was, filled a bucket of water from the well, and then stoked the wood under the stove to start a fire to heat the water, which she used for dishes and clothes.

Their home and farm were right out of a Norman Rockwell *Post* cover of America in the early 1900s.

We all pitched in to help her, but she was fussy and often told us to just go and relax, and enjoy nature. At night, if I had to go to the bathroom, I would get up, put on my shoes, and walk out back to the outhouse. There was no problem with the cold in the Amazon, but the toilet tissue was another challenge because there was none! Instead, my grandparents hung catalogs they received in the once-a-week mail on a wire; when you needed it, you just tore off a page. There were a few times when I just held it instead of going outdoors and sitting on that nasty, splintered bench to pee. Essentially, inside the outhouse was a plank of wood with a big hole cut in it that you sat on to do your business. The deep bottomless pit below was the most awful hole you can imagine! The smells with the heat and flies, and God knows what other bugs, was nearly unbearable. It was like something out of an old horror movie, and I suspected there were perhaps other strange creatures dwelling down there as well!

Since I often held it, I sometimes peed in the bed. My grandmother was a patient woman, but she drew the line with bed wetters. My bed was a cot with a three-inch-thick piece of foam on it. When I got it wet, she would move it and me out back with one of her comforters. However, instead of lying on the foam, she made me lie on the cot and then put the mattress over my head, pee and all. "I'm going to teach you not to pee the bed," she would say, but with a smile. Right away, I was learning a great deal.

Among the many things I remember was the heat; everything was hot or *very* warm. The well water was a little cool, but not by much. The milk was only slightly warm, because you took it right out of the cow when you needed it. There was no place to keep the extra, so any fresh milk disappeared quickly. There was no refrigerator and, of course, no ice, either; it seemed I was always craving a cold drink of any kind.

During the day, it was often 105 degrees which, combined with the 85-percent humidity, was like nowhere I'd ever lived up to that young age.

What I really liked was going out with my grandfather early in the morning to help him with his chores and learn all about nature and the animals. Sometimes I had to beg him because he felt some of the chores might be a little too much for a young city girl.

One day, he took me to a slaughter. Among the many animals they raised (horses, cows, chickens, and pigs), they would kill a cow periodically for the meat. It wasn't that often because they had no way of keeping it cold; everything had to be eaten relatively quickly or sold. That's when I learned there were milk cows and meat cows.

Grandfather would come up upon the animal quietly, though I sometimes suspected the cow knew what was about to happen, as it would get skittish and scurry away, making it necessary for him to traipse after it. When he got close, he took a long, very sharp knife and slit the cow's throat. The first time I saw him do it, I almost passed out. I remember the blood squirting everywhere like in the Freddie the chainsaw massacre movies. The big heavy cow would drop like a 1,000-pound bag of wheat to the ground. It was awful!

However, it was quick, and my grandfather assured me, painless, though I'm not sure that was true. When the throat was cut, the cow would gurgle for a split second, her eyes would roll back in her head, and then she slumped as if there wasn't a bone in her body.

Then, he would butcher the cow right there, showing me every step of what he was doing and which parts were which, because he used them all. I was getting a firsthand anatomy lesson I will never forget. After that, I no longer wanted hamburgers, but my grandparents ate the intestines, the brain—you name it; nothing was wasted. I think they even used the hooves for something.

The other animals used for all three meals were the chickens. We ate their eggs early and their breasts later. Grandfather had a special tree in the back that he used. He would snap the chicken's neck so fast you couldn't see his hands move, and then he would tie a piece of twine around one leg and hang the bird upside down.

"Grandpa," I said the first time, "why are you hanging it upside down?"

"So's all the blood will drain out and your grandma and you can clean it. You'll be pullin' out all the feathers so she can boil it for dinner," he told me.

Every day, a guy stopped by to take orders for beans or rice. My grandfather had a little market thing going on. He put out whatever he had, collected other vegetables from the surrounding farmers, and sold it all to this guy.

After a while, I was beginning to realize a system of sorts that worked well for them. They rarely wasted anything—and I mean anything. Whatever miniscule parts were left of the cow, or any other animal we didn't eat, were fed to the pigs (who, it seemed, could even eat aluminum).

I learned more about life that year working on the farm with my grandparents than I have since. They taught us about the environment, waste, the basics of running a farm, raising food and animals, bartering for goods, and all the other essentials one would guess could be learned in that situation.

My grandfather was also a very spiritual man. The three things I learned about him were: He loved his wife like no man before or since loved a woman; he had a strong faith in God; and he worked like a dog every day, though he didn't think of it as work.

He was also a philosopher and the local Pastor. More than anything, he wanted to teach me to find strength in God, which is one of the many things I learned from him.

The town had a very small church not far away that we walked to every Sunday morning to hear the sermons and sing the hymns; but Sunday wasn't a day of rest as it is in other religions; it was a working day just like any other. It seemed that my grandparents were in a perpetual motion machine where they had to keep the wheels spinning or else the whole system would crash, and it would be far too difficult to start again.

One of my favorite memories is my grandfather's tales. He was a master storyteller. He would spin great yarns and sagas about his childhood, about falling in love with my grandmother, and about growing up. His tales were far better than going to any movie theater, especially when he shared stories about my grandmother. I could tell by the sound of his voice and the look in his eyes that he was beyond devoted to her; he would have taken a bullet for her in an instant.

To my grandfather, my grandmother was the most beautiful creature on the face of God's earth. They had 13 children so you can imagine the stories they could both tell about the family. His love for her was beyond anything I had ever imagined, even with my Barbie and Ken dolls.

He had her firmly enthroned on a pedestal, which is where he kept her. The devotion and love between them was so strong, when they were in the same room, you could feel it—the electricity and some indescribable force of caring and well-being.

Grandfather also told me about his days in the Brazilian army. After he was discharged, he came back to his wife, started their farm, and the childrearing began in earnest. When a few of the kids got a little bit older, they would help with the younger ones, which would be repeated for more than 20 years until they were all grown.

Today, I have 22 cousins and I adore them all. We are all good friends but I avoid going to Brazil for Christmas because it is almost impossible to buy presents for all of them, and I wouldn't want them getting me gifts.

Later that summer on the farm, I was bitten by a mosquito. I'd been bitten plenty of times before, but this one was different. It was a Rondonian mosquito, and I contracted something called "fibromylia," which looked like chickenpox.

I became extremely ill but there were no doctors nearby. Even to use a phone, you had to somehow go into the city, which was miles away, and call an operator to put you through to a doctor. My mother went in the wagon with my grandfather. She called my Grandma Ercy who became very upset, blaming my mother for taking us out to the jungle. I remember her berating my mother. "What did you expect? I'm going to take her with me. I have the best insurance and the best doctors, and I'm going to raise her," Grandma Ercy said. I was her first-born female grandchild, so she favored me over the rest of the kids.

I was scared out of my wits when she took me to Rio that week. I had big boils all over my body that ached and itched. The only treatment was to get daily injections of some thick white liquid in a very large needle. They had to inject it into my buttock because my arms were too skinny. The shots hurt almost as much as the boils. To make matters even worse, I also had a terrible fever.

Every night, my grandmother would rub the lotion the doctor gave her on all my bumps and scabs every night. Most nights, I sat up in bed to keep from rubbing the sores. Eventually, of course, it went away and by the time it did, I felt like a pincushion with scabs, truly ugly, enough to scare the kids away in the new school. They thought I had leprosy.

I stayed with my father's mother in Rio while my family was still on the farm in Rondonia.

A FEW MONTHS AFTER MY illness, while still living with my grandmother in Rio, my father was released from jail in Florida on probation. Even though my family thought it was best for him to sell everything as originally planned so he could join us to start a new life in Brazil, he was not allowed to leave the country.

Grandma Ercy said, "Come to Brazil, your country. We will help you start over and you can live here, close to us." My grandfather insisted it would be best to just leave everything and start over. Since my father agreed, he didn't hesitate and went to Brazil with the intention of never going back to the U.S.

My paternal grandparents found us a house, and things were good for a while. Then, as it often does, life threw us another curveball: Grandpa Maia was diagnosed with cancer and became very ill. On top of that, my mother found out she was pregnant again. Her pregnancy with Evelyn had been wonderful. We lived normally and did normal things. We even took Tai Kuan Do classes through the first seven months of her pregnancy; but this time it was different because she was always feeling sick. She didn't know why but she felt sicker than usual, even more than the frequent bouts of being tired or feeling as though she had the flu.

It was time for me to really step up and help, so I learned how to cook and helped my mother with everything around the house. Since there were few construction jobs available, my father studied hard, got a real estate license, and was trying to get back on track; but even that was slow and though he worked long hours, he wasn't making any money. The bills were starting to overwhelm my grandmother, who was not only worrying about all of us but her husband as well because he was in the hospital fighting cancer while, simultaneously, my mother was going in and out of the hospital with her difficult pregnancy.

My sister, Raquel, was due to arrive at the end of July; but one night, during my mother's sixth month of pregnancy, she contracted a bad infection—putting both her and my sister at high risk. They were rushed to the hospital, where the doctors decided it was necessary to perform a C-section or she would lose the baby, so Raquel was born three months premature in 1996. She was tiny and sick so she was taken immediately to an incubator while my mother remained in the ER where they were trying to stabilize her. It was a very scary and sad time for all of us. No one could tell us if the two would be okay or would recover. It was the first time I'd ever seen my father cry.

I begged and prayed to God to save my mother. I stayed at the hospital and prayed for days. My father stayed as well. After several days had passed, he told me to leave, that he would stay by himself. It was important for me to take care of my sister, Evelyn, and to help my grandparents, he said.

Nevertheless, I visited my mother and Raquel every day. I'd walk to the hospital, which was about two miles from our apartment. After a lot of prayers and a long recovery, my mother was released two weeks later. However, my new baby sister, still fighting for her life, remained in the incubator, so that I had to watch her from behind the glass when I went to see her. She was incredibly tiny, about the size of a large fist, and the poor little thing had tubes coming out of her in every direction. I would tell her through the glass how much I loved her and couldn't wait for her to come home.

Finally, after two months, she was released and today she is healthier than any of us.

By the time Raquel was born, all of our money had run out. Everything is very expensive in Brazil, especially doctors and hospitals, not to mention prescriptions. Since my father was not making enough money to support us—and since he'd always been a proud man—despite the fact that he'd left the U.S. while on probation, he decided we were going back. He knew his way around there, especially in Florida and New York. Therefore, in his mind, the choice was simple.

When Raquel was about seven months old, we packed our things again and returned to the U.S. This time we went to New Jersey, where my father had friends and old associates, including my Godfather Lax, one of the largest builders in New Jersey and Queens.

We settled in quickly. It didn't take long for my father to get back on track and in just a matter of months he built a team of workers (his crew, as he liked to call them), and began his own construction company. My father worked like a plow mule and he made sure that the people around him worked just as hard; therefore, his business prospered rapidly.

Things were good for a little while. My father had a steady income and we were all together. Who could ask for anything more? Every weekend Dad took us to Chucky Cheese, our favorite place to go; and in the summer, we pursued numerous outdoor activities. No matter how hard my father worked, though, he always made time for us. He was home for dinner every night, and every weekend he would take us out somewhere special. Then, one night he didn't come home for dinner. He had been pulled over for a bad headlight and the cop ran his name. Since he'd violated his probation in Florida, there was an outstanding warrant for his arrest, which is when our real nightmare began.

My mother was now alone to raise three daughters and didn't have a clue what she was going to do without my father. At the age of 11, I had to step up and be there for her and my family.

It was 1997 and although my father had been arrested in New Jersey, he was transferred to Florida where the warrant had been issued.

Unfortunately, not understanding how to handle money and the many other things my father took care of, Mom made a number of mistakes.

WE MOVED AROUND A lot after that. I've lost track of how many there were, but it seemed I was forever the new kid in school. In middle school, I weighed 110 pounds, was skinny, had no breasts (which I wanted but should not have expected yet), and had a large butt. Nowadays, people assume I've had it "done" to mimic J Lo, but I haven't. It's all mine.

One of the nicknames I picked up was *"Tanajura,"* which is a Brazilian ant that is skinny but has a very large bubble behind. Or they called me "Chicken Legs," because I had thin legs and no chest.

Most of the older girls in school had good-size breasts, and I was jealous. I didn't want to wait to grow just a little at a time, so I took matters into my own hands, thinking the world would view me differently if I had boobs and looked more like the other girls. I actually thought that was the reason people picked on me. Even though it was all in my head, I was, as always, determined. There would be no stopping me. I was going to get some boobs one way or another. I had a plan.

I began to stuff my bra with toilet paper. My plan was to tell no one, *absolutely no one*. Gradually, I would add more until people began to notice that I was "growing." I started with just a little, folded over flat, and pushed it into my bra, then more folds, thicker paper, more folds—and *voila*!

I didn't even have the patience to wait a few months; I wanted breasts quickly, so made sure that I had beautiful large ones within two weeks. Although they hardly fit my skinny frame, they looked perfect to me. While I began to wonder why my mother hadn't noticed them earlier, I ultimately just assumed she thought they were growing naturally.

By then, I was using one of my mother's smallest bras. Behind my bedroom door, I would carefully shape the toilet paper like a breast, gingerly placing it upside down in the empty bra cup, carefully putting the bra on over my flat chest. It wasn't easy keeping it formed and in place all day, but it was worth it.

When I thought I was about as big as made sense for me to be, my mother confronted me one day as I was leaving for school.

"What are you doing?" she demanded to know.

"What?" I said innocently.

Without answering me, she pulled up my sweater, reached into *her* bra, and removed the wads of toilet paper.

I was mortified!

"You are making pretend breasts?"

"Mom, please don't make me stop. All the kids think I've grown them. If I go back to school without them, my life will be ruined, over, finished."

Silently, she gave me a stern look, making me sweat a little longer and then, unable to contain herself any longer, she burst out laughing and then kissed my forehead. "Suelyn, you must stop this. It is silly. Everyone probably already knows, but no one wants to hurt your feelings. Leave these out. You'll have what you want soon enough and then there will be boys and days when you wished you didn't have them at all."

"Okay, Mom," I said, secretly knowing I couldn't stop. I'd find a way.

Then came my moment of reckoning when a few days later, in the school cafeteria, I grabbed my tray and as I was walking to my table, the apple I had selected fell off my tray onto the floor. I bent down to pick it up, and one of my new fake toilet paper boobs fell out, next to the apple. I stood there, frozen in fear, with one boob still in place, the other lying on the hard linoleum floor.

My eyes darted around the room, hoping no one had noticed; but as I picked up the apple and the boob, someone called out, "Hey! Look at Suelyn; she's lost her paper boob."

Oh my God! My life was over in that instant. Kids started running over, climbing on chairs to get a better view. I wanted to take the plastic fork off the tray and stick it in my carotid artery.

Instead, I dropped the tray and ran, making a beeline to the bathroom, where I locked myself inside and started to cry uncontrollably. Then I heard a teacher knocking on the door. "Suelyn, lunch is over. You have to go back to class now," she said.

The thought of going to class at that point was alien to me.

"I'm not coming out," I yelled. Then there was silence and I was alone again with my misery for about ten minutes until a counselor unlocked the door and came in, searching the stalls for me.

"Aha! Suelyn, there you are. Your mother is on the phone; she wants to speak with you."

Oh boy; it was getting worse, much worse. My world was closing in on me like a giant vice. My mother would kill me; the kids would torture me forever. My picture would be in the yearbook, trying to pick up a toilet paper boob and I'd be on the news that night for sure.

I went to the phone and told my mother in Portuguese that my life was over and if it wasn't, I'd end it myself. "I need you, Mom," I said.

"Okay," she said, "I'm on my way. Stay where you are."

Within an hour, she picked me up. I never went back to that school again because, as it turned out, we would be moving soon and I would get a reprieve, a new school, and new friends who wouldn't know what had happened.

MY MOTHER NEVER FULLY recovered from the loss of my father, which is when she turned to the church, religion, and God.

At the New Jersey church, Pastor Jair and the people my mother called "brothers and sisters" received all of us with open arms. My mother shared her plight with the Pastor, who was very willing to give her advice on everything from raising us to the house and all of our belongings.

Pastor Jair used to preach, "Do for others and God will do for you." He had such an influence on my mother that she decided to dedicate her life to helping others by becoming a missionary.

The Pastor baptized her and gave her a missionary card. Within weeks, she was completely changed. She stopped using makeup, doing her hair, and getting dressed up. She began to cover every inch of her body with clothing. She believed it was all God's will, which, according to the Pastor, was our purpose in life.

After that, we were attending church five times a week and on Sundays, we would be there all day long. My mother would even cook and help clean the church whenever she could. My sisters and I went with her, of course, and helped in any way we could.

Unfortunately, God didn't help us with the mortgage and, according to my mother, that was okay with her, because that was God's will, too. She gave up worrying about the payments or fighting over the house, so we lost our home and stayed with one of the "sisters," Cristina, from the church.

Cristina had two children, so it was crowded in her small apartment with seven of us squeezed in, but we were grateful for the roof over our heads. Cristina's husband was also in jail, so she empathized with us and told us we could stay until we went to Brazil after my father's court appearance.

The church had a big warehouse full of donations, including clothing, toys, shoes, and household goods. My mother, always wanting to help others less fortunate, decided we were going to load up a container (a very large one) with some of the donations and take it with us to Brazil. Her plan was that once we arrived, other missionaries would distribute the things in the slums. It all made my mother feel great. She felt like she was helping to erase some of her sins, whatever those were.

When we finally left, my mother gave most of our things to the brothers and sisters in the church. She told us that we could pack one suitcase with our favorite things and gave the rest away, which was easier for my mother than it was for three young girls. What were our favorites? How could we leave so many things we loved? We would have nothing, but that was kind of her intent. She was definitely into minimalism, which she thought helped cleanse her soul. It just made us very sad. We were leaving everything. We'd lost our home, our father was in jail for doing nothing more than trying to catch the American dream, we owned no belongings anymore, and we were moving again. It wasn't one of the favorite times in my life.

However, my mother felt whole and for that I am grateful. My sisters and I, on the other hand, felt empty and adrift; but I was my mom's best friend and she mine, so that was that.

The church warehouse was an abandoned building behind the church, worn out and worn down with rotten wood siding. There were hundreds and hundreds of unmarked and uncategorized boxes and mountains of "stuff." There were shoes in with canned goods and dresses with teddy bears. The church just kept accepting the largess, stuffing it in boxes and shoving it in the warehouse.

Of course, my mother took it as her responsibility to organize it all, and so began the nightly treks to the warehouse to sort and organize. Many times, we just slept there. I would pick a mountain, climb to the top, and sort. Anything usable would be set aside. The torn, stained, nasty stuff went into big heavy lawn bags.

Once I'd whittled my way down the mountain a little, I'd take the "keepers" and use an old card table that we found to neatly fold, re-box, and then label with a Magic Marker.

Evelyn and Raquel tried to help, but they just seemed to make matters more complicated. Most of the time, they would play hide and seek with each other or if they found a usable toy, they would play with that. I don't ever remember getting any lunch during those days or the Pastor sending anyone else out to help us, but that was probably because my mother had told him that she would handle it by herself.

As we sorted and packed, Mom would pray aloud or sing hymns. After two months, we had one of those large steel ship containers filled to capacity with stuff to send to Brazil. When it was sealed and shipped, we were told it would arrive in five months, which would be just about the time we were going. The Pastor couldn't believe his eyes when he saw what we had accomplished. There were no more mountains, just well-organized and labeled boxes ready for shipping.

After that, perhaps a month later, my father's court date was finally nearing, so we flew from New Jersey to Florida to attend. I will never forget it as long as I live. We all sat in a courtroom in the first row and my father and an attorney sat at a table in front of a judge. After all the kibitzing and jostling of papers, the judge sentenced my father to seven years in jail, mostly because he had gone back to Brazil while he was still on parole for the first violation.

I thought about it long and hard. I would be almost 20 years old by the time I saw him again. I broke down in uncontrollable crying when the bailiff took him out the doors. It was as if my best friend was going to the gallows, never to be seen again. Would I even recognize him when we were finally reunited?

We stayed in Florida at a church with friends of Pastor Jair for a couple of weeks. They let us use the children's playroom. My mother and I slept side by side on nap mats laid out on the concrete floor, and my sisters slept in a crib. To keep ourselves entertained, we would play church in the main room where they held the services. Evelyn and I would turn on the microphones, sing, and play with the instruments. It was great fun. Isn't it wonderful how resilient children are? How they can create their own fun. That's something we lose as we become "adults."

We would all go to see Dad on Thursdays, which was visiting day. We did that every week until it was time to leave for Brazil, saying our goodbyes, which just brought forth more tears.

A few months after we arrived, the container we'd filled arrived, having been sequestered at Customs for quite some time. My mother finally managed to get it released using her missionary card.

With the help of our new Pastor, we were able to distribute all the clothes, toys, and household goods throughout Rio de Janeiro. We visited all the major slums, Favela da Galinha (the largest slum in all of South America) being our focus.

Having heard about us from the people in the neighborhood, we would find some high ground, open all the boxes, and prepare for the throngs who would show up. The Pastor would offer prayers for each person receiving something.

Though I was skeptical at first, I have to admit that my mother's devotion and discipline turned out to be a watershed period of my life. Having lost everything, including my father, here we were giving everything to others. It made me feel proud and good, and full of gratitude. When I saw the smiles on all those faces, particularly the small children getting toys, it nearly broke my heart—but in a good way.

CHAPTER TWO

Blossoming in Brazil

Whe n I was a little older, still living in Brazil, I became popular in school, but it wasn't always that way, which I like to think had more to do with my personality than my looks.

I was always gregarious and inquisitive, which made me a good listener—always wanting to learn something. I was interested in people, especially what made them tick or what motivated a particular person. Listeners are always popular. I was also attracted to science projects in school or how to play a sport better. I remember being highly competitive from an early age, which I think drove me to joining in all kinds of sports; and, to this day, I still am.

At 13, my body began to blossom. I had dangerous curves for such a young girl. I soon began to excel in sports, my grades got much better, and I was becoming proficient in three languages—and all the boys wanted to date me.

Funny how curves attract boys and grades attract teachers. I was popular with the male students and the instructors, but not so much with the girls.

Do you remember your first kiss? Perhaps not. Do you remember your first "French kiss"? Probably.

If you're like me, it probably wasn't anything like what you expected, if you even expected anything. A first French kiss is one of those things that sneaks up on you; a jittery boy decides he's going to give it a try and *bingo*, you've got a tongue down your throat.

It was the Christmas holidays, right after my father had been sentenced. My grandparents had a beautiful home in Rio with gorgeous things, and Grandma Ercy was very much into decorations.

She had bedding sets for weekdays and then another special set for weekends. Not only the beds changed appearance from week to week, but the curtains, towels—everything—had to match or at least complement one another. You know the type: They must have the open ends of the pillowcases facing out, away from each other, and all the towels must be earmarked for guests only, even if no guests are coming. My poor grandfather used to use his pants to wipe his hands most of the time, for fear of a stern retribution from my grandmother.

She was a perfectionist in her home and, oh boy, did she get into Christmas! I helped her decorate the entire house that year. She was the managing partner and I was the grunt. I brought in all the boxes, unpacked them, and sorted the tree lights from the "other" lights. I stacked the tablecloths neatly. I placed the tree decorations in a box of their own, ready to hang.

No room in the house was left untouched, including the bathroom. There were decorations upon decorations. There were cakes, pies, cookies, and gingerbread men. With the possible exception of the closets, you could not turn anywhere in the house without seeing Christmas.

Now that we were back, my grandmother had a helper and a partner, a more than willing decorating mate. I loved it. I wanted to learn and was amazed with the way she went about her passion. We spent three full days setting everything up, right up to Christmas Eve.

The rest of the family was about to arrive, which included my Aunt Adrienne (who was 17) and her boyfriend, Leandro (who was 18).

On Christmas day, my grandparents were in the kitchen and my aunt was taking a shower in preparation for the big dinner. I was in my room, about to go down the hall to the kitchen, when

Leandro whispered my name from a doorway. "*Psst*, Suelyn," he said in a hushed tone.

I turned around and said, "What?"

There was no answer, he just grabbed me, pushed me against the wall and began to kiss me, lips to lips, his lips on my cheeks, his lips on my lips again.

"Leandro, what are you doing?" I said, trying to pull away.

Then he pulled my head back to his face, pressed his lips to mine and oh my God, he pushed his considerable tongue into my mouth. I thought I was going to vomit. I couldn't move. He had locked one arm around my shoulders and his hand around the back of my head. Then he started wiggling his tongue around in my mouth. It felt like I'd swallowed a large, bald caterpillar. It was disgusting. Then, I guess as a reprieve, he pulled his tongue out and began sucking on my bottom lip. He was trying to devour me, starting with my face.

I finally managed to shake loose and run into the kitchen to my grandmother, who immediately detected fear in my expression (and perhaps a little saliva dripping off my chin!).

"What's wrong, honey? You look like you saw a ghost."

I shook it all off mentally, took a deep breath, and said, "Nothing, Grandma," and I gave her a little fake laugh for proof. "Is there anything I can help you with?" I asked, trying to change the subject.

"Yes, dear. Please put these on the table and then go get ready. Everyone should be here any minute."

I was lucky to have my own room at my grandparents', so I retreated to my shower. After I'd scrubbed my mouth about 15 times, I stood under the warm water, trying to figure out what had gotten into Leandro.

Why did this happen? Did I cause it? Should I tell? Who would I tell?

Should I tell my aunt?

I didn't want to spoil Christmas. That would be very inappropriate and put a real damper on the celebration.

We had a beautiful dinner. The table had been set for a king and queen. I'd never seen anything quite like it. However, my appetite was spoiled. Every time I thought about Leandro, I gagged quietly into my napkin.

The next morning, I told Aunt Adrienne what happened. She was a very insecure person, so I didn't know how she was going to deal with it. She was also jealous of me because she had such a difficult time controlling her weight, and I could seemingly eat anything and everything and stay the same. I think she had a love/hate thing going for me. Maybe hate is too harsh a word, but there was definitely tension, and along with that came the digs when she would say things to try and make me feel insecure. After all, insecurity loves company.

Even though she was only five years older than me, Adrienne was forever asking for advice, but only when no one else was around. I would listen and always give her my honest opinion but the minute Leandro or her friends came around, she would be dismissive and kick me out of her room or revert to being the "adult," treating me like a little kid who was underfoot. Nonetheless, I decided to tell her anyhow.

I went into the guestroom and stood, facing her. She stood quietly as I told her everything and then, her face expressionless, she left the room without saying a word. Later, she returned and called me back into the room. She grabbed my arm and said, "You're a liar and you know it. You like Leandro and you wish he was your boyfriend, that's why you're telling these tales about him, trying to seduce him. Why, you're nothing but a skinny little thirteen-year-old with no boobs or body. Why would he want you when he has me?"

I couldn't believe what she was saying. If it hadn't hurt so much, I would have burst out laughing at the absurdity of her statement.

"I don't want you to ever talk to him again, little niece. *Ever!* Do you understand? Now get out of here."

(By the way, I now know that this was just a part of growing up. Adrienne wasn't much older than I was; she subsequently grew out of her jealousy and is a happy, successful mother today.)

Of course, at the time, I was shocked and hurt. From that day until I was quite a bit older, I thought it best to just keep quiet about such things until I talked with older women, saw the news on TV, heard the stories of why so many women let their husbands abuse them, or why some never report a rape.

My thinking didn't change. I always told the truth when asked, but I never volunteered information, which I accomplished by defending myself before anything happened. Trust no one was my motto. At the end of the day, everyone has an agenda, not just men. I had been disappointed over and over again by uncles, cousins, teachers, Pastors, boyfriends—you name it. Betrayal is the worst action and emotion that exists.

It started when I was 7 in that bathroom and the look my Barbie dolls gave me. It continued with the Pastor who wanted to leave his wife for me, a child (which I talk about a little later), and it will continue to be "out there" if I allow it; but when I see that the road ahead is under repair these days, I take the nearest exit and use the surface streets.

AT 14, I WAS IN BRAZIL. My mother, two sisters, and I were living in Rio, and my mother's devotion to the church continued unabated after my father went to prison; in fact, she became a full-blown fanatic.

In the throes of her obsession with her religion, she continued dressing differently, very conservatively; almost a uniform, which consisted of skirts that nearly touched the floor and long-sleeved shirts (even during the hot summer months). Where once she wore leather sandals and nice heels of various colors, she now wore clunky, matronly shoes.

I wasn't particularly "religious," though I did believe in God through osmosis with my mother. Helping with Pastor Jair's warehouse and then giving away all the things we'd organized began my change of heart. However, the incident that pushed me further to follow in her footsteps happened shortly after we had been in our new apartment.

The area was a lower-middle-class neighborhood very close to a dangerous slum—Favela da Galinha—where one of the largest drug gangs ruled. The two-and-a-half mile walk to school every day took me on a harrowing journey through some of the most dangerous slums in Brazil where the drug lords ran everything, including the police.

It was a sweaty, dank, and dusty environment where, given the uncertainties of the streets, people stayed indoors as much as possible.

The kingpins or bosses unceremoniously and frequently chose young girls so they could make them "their women." Once a young girl, typically my age, was chosen, she was abducted, usually on the way to school. She was then taken to a secret place to bear the thug's children, never to be seen again. As these girls had no choice, they usually became one of the gang.

Since the families were powerless to do anything, they never searched for their missing daughters. To do so would risk their own lives, and they never called the police because they knew that was fruitless. So, the ultimate bullies ruled. They were dictators of their own fiefdoms, free to conduct drug sales at will and kidnap any young, attractive girl they took a fancy to from a practically unending supply.

Soon to be 15, I already had a curvaceous body like that of an 18-year-old. I was slim with nice breasts and a shapely rear end too large not to notice. My skin was like a pool of honey, and I had large brown eyes and full red, adult lips. I might as well have been a homing beacon.

For the first couple of weeks, my friends and I made the trek to school and back without incident until I heard a rumor that "Baby," the new drug lord, was asking questions about me. This alone was enough to send chills down my spine.

When my mother found out about this, with the exception of personally taking me to school and church, she kept me in the house 24/7—not that this diminutive woman could have fought off such a ferocious man's henchmen. However, after a period of time without incident, I was allowed to walk to school again. On that day, while taking a short cut down an alley, I was confronted by a large hulking man with very dark skin, a lot of tattoos, and several scars across his face. When he talked, his thick black handlebar mustache went up and down like an ugly caterpillar working its way up his face.

"Baby wants to see you," he said.

Knowing Baby's reputation, I nearly peed my pants. In defense, I could feel my skin begin to tighten and my fists clench. I knew that once I was in Baby's presence, I would never return home. I would become a sex slave and a baby mill just like all the other girls from the same neighborhood.

"Okay," I said as casually as I could muster. "But I have to go home first to change. I'm all sweaty from walking, and I want to look my best when we meet."

"Hah," the hulky guy guffawed. "You are a smart one. No, you will not go home. You will come with me," he ordered, stepping close enough for me to feel his breath on my face.

Think quickly. You must do something.

As he grabbed me, I turned and bit his forearm as hard as I could. When he recoiled in pain, I quickly kicked him in the groin, a move I'd learned in New Jersey in Tai Quan Do and then I took off running like a cheetah until I was many blocks away from him.

When I reached a busy public area, I ran into a supermarket and called my grandmother.

As I spoke with her breathlessly, I could taste the vile man's blood and sweat in my mouth from when I bit his arm. I hadn't called my mother because my grandmother lived an hour away in a nice neighborhood and I was afraid we would be followed home.

We stayed with her for a week longer and then packed up every stitch of clothing and belongings we had and moved to Alcantara, a city three hours away.

Coupled with that experience, being as close as I was to my mother and adoring her the way I did, I followed her lead and immediately took an even stronger interest in church, though I didn't dress as strictly as she did.

I got to know the Pastor, who took an interest in me and soon became a man I greatly respected. At the age of 14, he put me in charge of the children's Bible school and encouraged me to sing in the choir. Soon, I was nearly as devoted to the church (not to necessarily be confused with Christianity) as my mother. I believed everything the Pastor said, all his quotes from the Bible, his stories, and his rules. I learned it was a sin to have sex before marriage. I learned that if I kept myself pure, God would choose a man for me and, together, we would be blessed (and then it would be okay to make love).

Not only was I a firm believer, but I often fasted to help keep impure thoughts out of my mind and temptations at bay. Later that year, I would be celebrating my birthday. In America, we celebrate the 16th birthday as a Sweet 16 event. In Brazil, that happens at age 15. Raquel was turning 5 on April 30th, Evelyn was going to be 7 on May 12th, and my birthday was on May 14th, all within two weeks of each other; so instead of having three parties, my parents decided to have one big Sweet 15 party for the three of us.

The party was to begin just after Sunday services. However, that morning, the Pastor summoned me to the church early. He'd sent a note indicating that he had something important to tell me before my birthday party and asked me to come in early. Eager to please one of my heroes, I arrived an hour before the services were scheduled to begin.

When I pushed open the large wooden doors, I heard a quiet voice from the back of the church. "Suelyn. Back here. Come back here."

Although I couldn't see him, I recognized the Pastor's voice and followed the echoes down a hallway behind the pulpit and stage.

It was dark in the hall, but I could make out the Pastor's figure. He approached me, gave me a big hug, and said he had a message for me from God, and then he added, "Happy sweet fifteen."

He put his arm around me and we began to walk down the hall to his office where he pushed open another enormous door to his inner sanctum filled with religious artifacts: crosses, candles, gold chalices and, of course, a large open Bible resting on a pedestal.

"Suelyn," he said, "I have had a message from God about *us*. Please sit." I was immediately intrigued and sat down in a red leather chair, waiting with baited breath for his devout message.

"Suelyn, God has told me that you are *my* chosen one and I am *your* chosen one."

As he paced rather nervously in the room in front of me, before he could continue, I stood to speak, but he admonished me to stay seated until he was through with God's message. This was not the message I was waiting for; frankly, I'm not sure what news I thought I was going to get, but I knew *this* wasn't it.

"Suelyn, this means God has blessed us and that we must be together. We must get married right away."

Huh?

His words were so foreign, so out of context, so embarrassing and preposterous to me, for a split second I thought he was joking, but quickly saw in his expression and sensed in his voice that he was quite serious.

As he continued to pace, his hands grasping each other behind his back, I remained speechless.

"Suelyn, my dearest, you shall be my wife and you will have my children."

Finally able to catch my breath, I asked, "But Pastor, what will become of the wife and children you already have?"

His answer was quick and decisive, "Oh, that. They will be fine. God will provide for them. You and I can leave this town and start fresh somewhere else. God will follow and bless us."

It was as if I was speaking with a lunatic, a person who had just imploded for whatever reason, and gone off the deep end of reality.

"Pastor, with all due respect," I said as I stood and began to back away, "I don't think you were speaking with God." With that, I bolted for the closed door and ran all the way home in tears. When I got there, my mother was getting ready to leave for church, all made up in a long black dress and a black lace veil, which would have been more appropriate for a funeral. I raced past her, went into my room, locked the door, and threw myself on the bed. After several knocks and a loud monologue about my not going to church and how the devil was to blame, she gave up and left with my sisters.

I cried all that morning. It was my first real taste of betrayal, to my mind the worst sin imaginable. I had looked up to this man as though he were a saint. He was one of the few people outside my family that I trusted implicitly. He was safe and protective, or at least I thought he was.

Baby wasn't a betrayal. He acted his chosen role out to perfection. Likewise, my father's worker was just plain evil; but the Pastor was far more insidious because he hid his wickedness behind God. Baby was at least honest to form, whereas the Pastor was devious and scheming.

From that day forward, I never went to church again, for which I blamed only one man. I did learn three valuable lessons, however: Do not put humans on a pedestal; they are too frail. Do not put men on pedestals; they are the frailest of the frail; and, no one is better than you are.

On my 15th birthday, I learned to always use common sense and not to form mentorships carelessly. I also learned to pay more attention to my intuitions—those nagging thoughts we often fail to heed—and to have more respect for the brains God gave me.

After the experience with the Pastor, you'd think I would have learned. After just writing about my lessons (common sense, frailty, trust, and religion), those lessons didn't truly sink in for a while. Then, I was confused and very disappointed in the church and the people who ran it.

I don't know if it was my hormones, a natural new stage in growing, the curiosity of a teenage girl, or just rebellion, but I slowly began to dress in more revealing clothes. I replaced my common sense with my basic physical urges. Just like the teenage boys around me, my thoughts drifted further and further from the scriptures and moved more and more toward giving my body what it was asking for.

Losing My Virginity

A s mentioned earlier, I was very popular in school and most of the boys wanted to date me, but I found them all boring and immature, even the seniors. I didn't have the patience for their . . . well, their "boyish ways." Then one day, while my family and I were at the beach and I was about to walk into the ocean to cool off, I saw an angel in the water. His image was like a wave knocking me over. Wading out of the white water in my direction was, I would later learn, Gabriel—tall, dark, piercing blue eyes; blue enough that I could clearly see the color from 20 yards away.

With broad shoulders, a six-pack, and gorgeous skin, he was built like a swimmer. I had to catch my breath for a second as he got closer. He wasn't looking at me, so I don't know if he whipped his long black wet hair just for me or because it was soaked, but the effect was like a shock of electricity.

I stood frozen, ankle deep in the water until he passed. I was still breathing heavily like you do when you're about to faint and someone tells you, "Breathe. Breathe deeply and slowly."

I immediately went into a dream state like in one of those old movies where the beautiful girl is running from one end of the beach and the handsome man is running from the opposite direction, and then they suddenly go into slow motion with their arms reaching out for each other. In the movie, her breasts are swaying in her napkin-size top, and the muscles in his loins and torso are taut and ready to spring into action.

It was too late to try to catch his attention, so I waited for a couple of seconds and then returned to my towel next to my cousin, Dayane, who could tell immediately that something was up. I picked up my towel and used it as an excuse to peek around as I dried myself off. I was wearing a very small, green-string Brazilian bikini. As soon as I was dry and had spread my towel out again, I shook and whipped my likewise long and silky black hair around, just in case *he* was looking.

I didn't see him, so I sat down, still not talking to Dayane, who was turned over on her stomach. Laboriously and meticulously, I began smoothing tanning oil over the muscles in my legs and arms, all the while glancing around, but he wasn't to be found. He had vanished like a ghost.

Sigh.

"What are you doing?" Dayane said as she turned over.

"What do you mean?" I said.

"You're preening like a peacock," she said, sitting up quickly and darting her eyes around the beach. "Where is he?"

"Where is who?" I asked innocently.

"Oh come on, girl. Where's Adonis?"

I tried to pretend that I thought she was crazy, but she knew better. There was a second's silence and then we both started to crack up and giggle, and make all those funny sounds that teenage girls make when their hormones begin to climb up their legs and their hearts start pounding.

Fate wasn't kind to me that day. Angel was gone, probably never to be seen again. *Why didn't I say something when I had the chance?*

Summer was still in full swing. It was hot and, with a little prodding from me, the family decided to go to the beach again the following Saturday. Dayane came along. She couldn't get off the past weekend, asking four or five times, "Is that him? Is that him? How about him?" she kept saying, pointing to various good-lucking young guys.

"No. No, and no," I kept saying. "And quit bugging me. He probably was just visiting town."

Out to the water we pranced and began splashing each other like little kids. Since we weren't paying attention, a wave about three-feet high shot up out of nowhere and knocked me down. Scrambling to get my bearings, I looked up and there he was, towering over me;

my Angel. Gabriel, my hero. He extended his hand with a big grin and said, "Here let me help you, Esther." I didn't know who Esther was, but later learned he was trying to be humorous by referring to the actress/swimmer, Esther Williams.

I smiled anyway, letting him know I "got it," and stood up while still clinging to his hand. He smiled again and now I could see them: the whitest, straightest teeth I'd ever seen in my entire life—so much so, they almost looked fake. They were so stunning, they were downright sexy.

Then I realized I hadn't let go of my death grip and he was trying to pull his hand away. I tried to be witty, funny, or at least sexy, but the words sputtered out, "Did . . . did you have braces?"

He smiled. "No. But thanks for the compliment."

Oh my God. I felt like diving under the very next wave so I could resurface about a mile down the beach!

Dayane wanted to give me space, but she also wanted to be introduced, so while I stood transfixed on Angel, she kept signaling me behind him, as if to say, "Come on. Don't be a pig. Introduce me."

"Weren't you here last week?" he asked.

I was stunned that he remembered; certainly a good sign.

My "yes" came out more like an "aw shucks" from an old Andy of Mayberry show. I finally managed to pull myself together and said, "Yes. This is our favorite spot. We come here every weekend."

"Well," he responded, "now it's my favorite spot, too."

There was a pregnant pause because I couldn't stop staring at his eyes and teeth.

"Are you coming next weekend?" he asked.

I wanted to say, "A team of wild horses couldn't keep me away," but instead, as I was trying to formulate a reply, he said, "Can I give you my number? I would like to get to know you better."

Since it hadn't been two months since the incident with the Pastor, I apparently hadn't learned my lesson yet, but I didn't care.

"I don't have a pen."

"I know," Dayane said, coming to the rescue. "Let's go to our towels. We can use my lipstick."

Yes! What a pal! I would never have thought of that.

When we got to our towels and Dayane pulled out her bright red lipstick, Angel said, "What can we write on?"

Again, Dayane to the rescue. "Here, use Suelyn's T-shirt."

After writing my number, I asked, "What's your name?"

"Gabriel," he answered, which I also thought was very sexy, *sort of like a movie star's name.*

Not wanting him to think I was too interested, I waited what I thought was a respectable amount of time—one day—and then I called him. To my surprise, he was happy to hear from me and didn't waste a minute asking me to go with him to a movie in the city. After a thoughtful couple of seconds, I, of course, said yes, even though I knew my mother would never let me go—but I'd worry about that later.

I needed a plan and came up with one quickly. I would enlist the help of my Aunt Adrienne and Dayane. Adrienne was 20 so I knew my mother would be okay with it. The plan—as is so often the case with diabolical teens who want their way—was to say I was going to Aunt Adrienne's for a movie. She had plans but after I described Gabriel to her, she agreed to cover for me. She accompanied us to the theater (only because she wanted to see Gabriel), talked the usual pleasantries, and then left to get on with her own plans.

When she was gone, as is fairly common in Brazil, Gabriel gave me a box of chocolates and flowers. When I told him that Dayane would be watching the movie with us, he said, "Oh, I'm sorry. Had I known, I would have brought her flowers as well."

When the movie was over and Dayane and I were ready to walk home, Gabriel turned, and without touching me, attempted to give me a kiss. I quickly turned my head so he could kiss my cheek.

A few months passed. We went to the beach often and saw an occasional movie together but then he told me he had to leave. He was in his first year of Army service and had to deploy in a week.

I was sick. It was such a surprise. Besides, Carnival was set to start in two days, which is the wildest, most celebrated holiday in Brazil. People come from all over the world to Rio just for that week's celebration of sun, fun, and debauchery.

Carnival week is also a great time for sales at all the stores, and I was starting a job selling dentistry equipment. Dealing with so many men (nearly all the dentists were male) taught me much about how to deal with them. Since I was closing in on my 16th birthday, I was quickly learning how to use my looks to my advantage while selling drills, bits, brushes, and all the other paraphernalia that dentists use.

I had to see Gabriel again before he left, and those days were dwindling. Therefore, I asked my mother if I could go shopping at the sales for some new work clothes but, of course, I was going to rendezvous with Gabriel.

The movie theater was closed that day, so Gabriel suggested we just go to his house. He lived five blocks away with his mother. The only snag in our plan was that *she* was home. And, he told me, she was *very* protective of him. She called him Baby, which sent a shudder down my spine.

"I don't mind, if you don't," I said.

"Neither do I. Come on; let's go."

When we got to his house, his mother acted as if he'd been off to war for a year, while I got a very icy reception. She'd never met me before, but my instincts told me that even if she had, her expression would have been the same.

We stepped into a small living room area with old, almost antique furniture. Even though it was hot out, she had all the windows closed and most of the drapes, so it was very stuffy.

Gabriel showed me to the couch and told his mother that we were going to go to the movie but it was closed. Sitting down next to him, she said, "Oh good. Then we can all sit together and chat." I groaned inside.

"Mom, Suelyn and I are going to my room to watch a movie."

Over my dead body, her face said.

"Why don't we all watch one together here in the living room," she offered, patting Gabriel on his shoulder.

Gabriel took a deep breath and said, "Mom, if you don't mind, we would like some privacy. We'll watch a movie in my room."

His mother's face melted like a grilled cheese sandwich without the toast and then just as quickly turned to a scowl. Inside, my heart was jumping and tumbling over and laughing—*yes! You tell her, Gabriel!* I was smart, though; I kept what would grow into my poker face at a later age by showing no signs of emotion, not even a blink.

With that, Gabriel stood, reached over for my hand, and off we went to his room. On a shelf next to his bed, along with quite a few books, were pictures of him in his uniform. As he told me about each one, he explained that he was a shooter and that his father had taught him. His stories had me mesmerized. After only a few, he patted the bed next to him, told me to make myself comfortable, and began to search the channels for a movie. Once he found one, he settled on the bed beside me, put his arm around me, and immediately started kissing me.

End of story. We never did watch the movie. He was a sweet, handsome, gentle man and when his hand finally slid up my dress, I almost passed out from ecstasy. Even though I envisioned his mother with her ear and a glass pressed up against the other side of the door, I kept encouraging him as I kissed him back as passionately as a young virgin knew how to do.

The sad, sad truth, however, is that after all was said and done, there were no explosions, no sparklers going off, no bells, no whistles. In fact, despite how sexy Gabriel was to look at and hold, the actual "act" was quite disappointing. I didn't let on, though. Instead, a few moments after we had finished, we got up and showered together.

Gabriel took me home on his motorcycle. As we pulled up in front of my place, he turned off the motor, I got off, he pulled off his helmet, and said, "Suelyn, I want you to be my girlfriend. I would like to ask your parents if I can be your boyfriend."

He'd taken me by surprise but I said, "Well, do you want to date me or my parents?" He laughed and then I said, "Let's talk about it tomorrow," and with that, I ran inside.

It wasn't 15 minutes before the phone rang. It was Gabriel.

"I would like to meet your parents before I go away," he said.

I stammered for a moment. "Well, my father is still away," (which was the truth). "Let's wait until he gets home."

As soon as I hung up, the guilt got the better of me. *What have I done? I lost my virginity today—something I prayed and believed in keeping for the man I loved, my life partner, my mate. Now it's gone, as easily as a melting ice cube in the hot sun. Why did I do this? I am only 16 and look at what I've done. It wasn't even worth it; there were no incredible feelings* (not that a great experience would have softened my guilt).

I learned in church from Pastor Jair in New Jersey that if I saved myself for my chosen man, God would bless me to be happy forever. My husband would love and protect me, and would be there for me until the end of my days, for better or for worse. We would take care of each other into our old age or until we died.

I was beyond redemption. My guilt and remorse were so strong, I could scarcely bear it. As I laid on my bed, my head buried in my pillow, feeling sorry for myself, I remembered the Pastor who'd made a pass at me, the one who was a married man of God with a loving wife and two daughters, the man who told me *he* was my chosen one. I was to marry him. He would drop everything to be with me. Was this his plan from the very beginning? He taught me all those things only to make sure I would remain pure for him. Now, I could add disgust to my guilt and remorse.

It made me think of when I was a small girl and my mother told me stories of how my father was her first and only. I'd witnessed her love and obsession for him all my life. She did everything for him as he did for her.

So now, I have lost my virginity and I will never deserve all those things the Pastor preached? Will I ever deserve a man who loves me and will be my equal? How can I believe anything I've learned from all these "wise" people? What is love anyway? I asked myself these questions that for a very long time. All I saw were women giving up everything for the men they loved to then be left years later for a younger, shinier showroom model.

I was learning through my guilt and remorse that all these men who made/make passes at me are married, religious, and are/or fakes, living counterfeit family lives.

I don't want to be the woman that's left all her dreams behind and sacrificed everything for the man she loves, only to be cheated on, beaten, or both, and then tossed aside for a younger woman.

Nevertheless, it wasn't Gabriel's fault. He was a gentleman, albeit one with strong hormones; but if I'd said no, that would have been the end of it, at least for the time being. So I dated him until he had to report to the Army. During that time, my father was released from jail in the U.S. and deported so, needless to say, we were excited to have him home. There was much to catch up on, plus we had to adjust to living as a family again because he'd been gone for four years.

I was no longer a child. Things were different and everyone had changed in small ways, including my father who now had to reorient himself to a real and very different world. After 9-11, many things had changed. We could only imagine the stories he could tell us about prison, but we never asked and he was always quiet about his experiences.

Later, Gabriel came back from the Army on leave and met my parents, and we began dating again on the weekends and in the early mornings.

Aside from a few hours on Saturdays, I didn't have permission to date then, and I didn't want to worry my parents, so Gabriel would pick me up at 4:00 a.m. so we would spend time together, then he would drop me off at school.

At the time, there was very little work for my father in Brazil. We had no money and things were getting more and more difficult by the month for all of us. When it got unbearable, without thinking it through, he called us all together and said we were going back to the U.S. because at least there was work there. We sold everything and set out on yet another journey.

I never forgot that night because I lost everything. From that moment forward, I thought about love a lot, which I supposed was just more fuel on the fire I had built of being jaded.

The only true love of lasting duration I'd ever witnessed was how Grandfather Lucas loved my Grandmother Maria. They met when they were teens and were married for over 60 years. They had 13 children and battled throughout their entire lives to raise and provide for them.

I saw that my grandfather was a man of God. He preached in his way, and I listened. Even when I didn't totally understand him at such a young age, I always knew he was wise. He taught me how to pray and, more importantly, how to have faith. I never told him my secrets but, if I had, I suspect he would have forgiven me. The year I lived with them in Rondonia in the Amazon jungle, my grandfather also taught me how to respect others and how to demand that same respect; and that it was important to respect your parents always, no matter how wrong their choices.

As we used to walk in the cane fields, he would share verses from the Bible with me. He had them memorized. He said, "filha," God is first in spirit, but on earth your grandmother is first. I will cherish her forever."

I nearly cried when he told me that. I thought, *That's what I want. Is he the only man in the world like that? Did God throw away the mold after he made Grandfather Lucas? Did my grandmother receive that love because she had no sin, because she saved herself for him? Have I thrown all that away? My God, what have I done?*

Is Gabriel really "the one"? But even as I thought it, I knew better.

Dear Journal:

(Note to self: Use this if you ever write a book.)

Introspection

(This was originally written in my code language)

@ ^^ # ^^ *&%* (**@~~~@ ##^^^##@9 *)__++
##@^^^%%%6 **^^—) 00 {{{# @@!!.

I don't think of myself as being special. I'm not any better or worse than anyone else is. Many children are scarred at a young age and, of course, many grow up in dysfunctional environments. Most turn out okay, regardless, because children are so resilient and far more intuitive and in the present than parents, family, and friends give them credit for.

Young children are like little spies among us—absorbing details, nuances, emotions, and cues from everything around them. Most children learn to use their entire environment to travel the best path possible, which includes all the positive and negative.

In my immediate family, there was a great deal of love (although my parents were at times pretty dysfunctional, if you take into account my father's incarcerations and his and my mother's drug use).

I took the best of both, though. From my mother, I saw and experienced her weaknesses, her need for my father to always protect and blaze new paths. I love her unconditionally and with great devotion, but I chose early on not to incorporate her emotional frailty into my own personal movie. Instead, I suppose I saw the fairy tale princess in her, the one who was always depending on her Prince Charming (fortunately, like Cinderella, she didn't have to spend a lifetime looking for him). Perhaps that's why I surrounded myself with so many Barbie Doll "friends" when I was young. (By the time I was 8, I had over 200 "babies," Barbies, including all the accoutrements of that make-believe life—Barbie cars, boats, clothes, jewelry, etc., mostly given to me by my father.)

My movie started early. I was the star, the director, the producer, and the audience all rolled into one. It wasn't until later I learned that's really how life works. We all create our own lives.

However, at a very young age (and this may have been a factor driving me to my Barbie world), I was hurt, lied to, and betrayed by the very people I trusted and cared about the most. So, as a consequence, I grew up learning to defend myself by not trusting anyone. I created a shield out of pure emotional survival needs—an attitude that led me slowly but ever so directly to a distancing mechanism: I always expected the worst and was rarely disappointed. I was jaded at a very early age. To protect myself, I kept people out. However, I learned to love and get along with most everyone, to have good times, but to always be on the alert, both eyes and ears wide open, hypersensitive of people's motives. It seemed, particularly with men, that the more generous, friendly, and caring they seemed to be at first, the deeper were their bad intentions.

Later, of course, as I got older, I realized what a heavy, heavy burden it was to carry this around. I remember playing with my "babies" a lot, using them as actresses to create the antithesis of my real world (I rarely owned Ken dolls and the few I had were only decorations for my girls). Through them and that role-playing, I became proficient at convincing people to trust me and share things, all the while pretending to share with them. I knew my sisters' and my friends' secrets, but they never knew mine—at least not my real ones.

But it didn't end with dolls. My mother would read to me every chance she got. I grew up on Dr. Seuss, but I was especially voracious for the fairy tales, which were always my favorites: Cinderella, Beauty and the Beast, Pocahontas, Little Mermaid and, of course, the movies that followed whenever Mom would take me.

My mother was very creative. She wrote a lot of poetry, which I also gobbled up. While my father was at work, interspersed with her cooking and cleaning, she would read and play with me. We had dress-up time and afternoon teas and when she wasn't playing with me, or I wasn't playing with my dolls, I would talk to my imaginary friend, Jennifer. My mother played with her, too—sometimes they even had fights. We would both blame her for anything I did wrong, like spilling things or not doing my chores—in other words, she was my "out."

Mom always told me I was smart and independent, so she would let me pick out my own outfits, even when I was only 4 years old. She told me this story from time to time about when we would go shopping and I would beg her to let me buy just about everything in sight. She would tell me she was out of money and I would ask her to put it on Daddy's "card." That almighty, magic piece of plastic meant you didn't have to have any money.

One day, after my father had been giving me dolls almost weekly for a year or so, it was time, according to him, to build a big bookcase to keep them in—and so he did. I loved him for that because then, I could see all my friends and players at a glance. Of course, they all had names, and I loved talking to them. They were my captive audience. They couldn't disagree, argue, or hurt me.

End of journal entry.

I LOVED EVERYTHING ABOUT MY Dad. He doted on me in different ways than my mother did. I wasn't spoiled, but I don't ever remember getting spanked. He once told me that when we were at the store one day, a lady came up to him to ask for directions. Though I don't remember it, I got jealous and kicked her on her shin, saying in a loud voice, "Daddy, it's time to go! *Mommy* is waiting for us."

My mother also told me stories about my young self. When I was 4, she and I were at the mall in a store and I suddenly disappeared which, of course, scared the wits out of her.

After 15 minutes of frantically searching half the mall, she returned to the store where I jumped out from behind a display and yelled, *"Boo!"* She said she came a foot off the floor and I thought that was just about the funniest thing I'd ever seen—so funny, in fact, that I continued throughout my young life to hide and scare her, about which she was always a good sport.

CHAPTER THREE

The Tony Years

WE HAD JUST MOVED from Brazil where my father was again arrested at the airport by immigration. Mom, my sisters, and I lived with Aunt Martha, who was living in Queens, until we rented a small apartment nearby on 38th Street and Ditmars. I was 16 but looked more like 18 or 19.

The New York borough of Queens is nothing like Manhattan. To me, it was dull, lifeless, and gray. It was decidedly one of the low-rent districts of New York. I wouldn't really know that, however, until I began to go to Manhattan.

That summer, by lying about my age, I got my first job at a Diesel Clothing Store. They paid me under the table, so there were no taxes involved and, of course, they could pay me less than a full-time employee.

I stocked shelves, took inventory, and sold jeans. One day, while on my lunch break, I was sitting on a park bench with my cousin who worked at Steinway's, another store close by, when a handsome man approached and sat at a distance at the other end of the bench.

After sitting quietly for a moment, he turned to me as I was biting into my ham sandwich and said, "Hello. My name is Tony. What's yours?" Since I was sitting closest to him, I assumed he was talking to me.

"I'm Suelyn," I said, that being the extent of my conversation as my cousin and I looked at each other and giggled.

After making small talk, he abruptly got serious and said, "I would love to take you out for drinks and dinner."

I was stunned. Certainly, I didn't think I looked old enough for alcohol and, at any rate, I wouldn't have had anything to drink anyway, but I was intrigued a bit as my cousin kept surreptitiously poking me in the ribs, smiling, and nodding in the affirmative.

It was a warm day, but not too hot, and there was a gentle breeze wafting about us. My lunch break was just about over and as I looked at the leaves shimmying on the branches around me and then back to Tony's dark, dark brown eyes, I began to think: *Why not? It might be fun.* Though he could have been the Son of Sam, the breeze, which was coming from his direction, brought the smell of something delightful. I later learned it was his cologne, something Italian, just like him. Since I liked it, my instincts told me I was safe.

Within a minute, he once again invited me to dinner. My cousin and I giggled, she prodded me, and I said, "Sure. When?"

A few nights later, he took me to a nice Italian restaurant and when the waiter came up, without asking me, he began to order drinks. I waved him off quickly, telling him I didn't drink and I sure didn't want the waiter asking for my ID.

The evening was pleasant and he was a complete gentleman, wanting to know everything about me. When the evening was over, he took me home, gave me a little hug (no kiss, which I didn't want anyhow), and then he was off in his black Mercedes.

It wasn't like I was smitten with Tony, or even that interested. He was simply a good-looking, well-mannered, well-dressed young man. He didn't call for several days. Finally, the messages started coming six days later, when he would read me poems and leave sweet messages.

A bit reluctantly, I finally answered him, even though I was only mildly interested. I'd just left my boyfriend (Gabriel, the one to whom I had lost my virginity) in Brazil and wasn't that enthusiastic. I certainly did not want to jump into a relationship at that point, plus I was really only 16 (even though I was getting accustomed to being 18 or 19 in my mind), and he was seven years older.

After giving it some thought, I decided I would see him again. We met at the park several times and he'd walk me to the Baskin-Robbins for ice cream or we'd go out to dinner.

Three dates later, I was beginning to feel a little safer when he suddenly asked, "Can I meet your parents? I'd like to take us all out to dinner."

Huh?

Boy, that quickly changed the complexion of things. Only three dates and he already wanted to meet my parents? Most American guys don't *ever* want to meet your parents, not even after you're married (kidding, of course).

"My father," I lied, "is off, away at work."

He was quick, answering with, "Well, then I'd like to take you and your mother." Then he smiled and waited for my response.

"Now would not be a good time," I said.

Tony told me he was half-Italian and half-Dominican, with a little Irish thrown into the mix for flavor. (He wasn't too good with math, which was strange because he would later become a stockbroker—*on second thought, maybe that wasn't so strange after all.*

I was beginning to see a very classy and caring guy until he added, "I'd really like to meet your mother and tell her I'd like to be your boyfriend."

Oh my God! He was moving way too fast and although so polite and caring, I should have seen the red flag then; but, of course, I didn't.

That's when I told him I wasn't 18. I even showed him my passport. I figured if he was going to talk to my mother, sooner or later she'd spill the beans anyway. As we walked from the restaurant back to the park, I said, "I have something to tell you, something I've been lying about."

He sat down on a nearby bench, pulled me down next to him, took two very deep breaths with a mildly fearful expression, and said, "Okay. What is it? I'm ready for anything."

I hummed and hawed, having second thoughts.

"Come on. Out with it. You're married, aren't you?"

"No. No, absolutely not."

"You have children? You just escaped from jail and don't work for Diesel?"

"No. No. And I'm not pregnant," (although I still hadn't even kissed him yet). "I lied about my age. I'm really only sixteen," I said, covering my face with my hands. I had my passport in my purse (just in case), so I pulled it out and handed it to him.

"I'm sorry, Tony. I'm really sorry. I just didn't think about it when we met."

I waited for his response. He sat quietly, staring straight ahead. I could see the wheels turning in his mind.

"Well," he finally said, "you are very mature for your age, and I don't have a problem with that. In Italy, it's normal and I'm sure it's not so out of the ordinary in Brazil, either."

Now, I no longer had a reason to worry about him meeting my mother and her telling him my real age first. The only thing I feared was that she would tell Tony about my father being in jail. I knew that eventually I would have to tell him, but right now it was too early, too soon in the relationship and, to be honest, after only three dates, I wasn't 100-percent certain we'd still be dating a month from today.

IN BRAZIL, HIGH SCHOOL is only three years long, so I'd already graduated before returning to the U.S. again. Along with introducing Tony to my mother, and all that would eventually entail,

I was working almost full-time at Diesel and wanting so badly to go to college where I could transfer my credits from Brazil. After applying to several colleges, I was accepted at Hunter in Manhattan. My only decision was whether to start right away, that semester, or wait for a few months. I decided to wait a few months.

My dream was to eventually go to medical school. In the meantime, Tony was ever-present. He was charming, family-oriented, and shared many traditions with me. I met his family soon after he met my mother (who did not tell him about my father). Tony was trying to become a stockbroker and had just received his license, but he still needed a job, which he managed to land quickly on Wall Street with a company called Raymond James.

Everything went well for about nine months. My mother liked him, and he was doing very well at his job. I was still living with my mother, and he had an apartment in Queens. Then, as quickly as it had all started, it looked like it would come to a screeching halt. Mom decided he wasn't right for me, not good enough for me: too many missed curfews, him wanting to take me on long trips to Florida, I was too young. Everything began to change, and then I met Brian.

There was a big parade that day in the city where I'd gone shopping. I'm still not sure what the celebration was for, but I stopped and watched for a while like most other people. Everyone loves a parade.

As a band marched by playing some tune, a guy with a camera in—hand and another hanging around his neck approached me.

"Pardon me," he said. "My name is Brian. I'm a photographer. Are you a model?"

Oh boy. I'd heard that one before. I drifted off for a second. It reminded me of something my grandfather in Brazil had told me. He'd said after I'd been in a small (very small) beauty pageant, "Suelyn, never use your beauty to succeed. Use your brains because they are your treasure."

Handing me a card, Brian yanked me out of my memories. "I'm a photographer—really," he said. "I know you've heard that before, but that's only because you're so attractive. If you ever feel like doing any modeling, give me a call—really, I'm legitimate."

I was guessing Brian was gay because he was quite effeminate in his speech and gestures. Turns out I'm still not certain if he's gay, straight, or bisexual.

Brian left to catch up with the parade, and I put his card in my purse. When I got home, I hid it, thinking: *Who knows?* I'd gotten cards from people who had clothing lines, did fashion shows, a lot of different things. I knew Tony went through my things, so it was imperative to hide them.

Over the next few days, I began to think about modeling. I couldn't get it out of my head. I don't know why, because I was focused on school and hadn't given it any thought before Brian approached me. For some unknown reason, maybe it was meant to be.

I'd always liked doing family pictures where I would be the one posing and everyone would tell me how cute my pose was. I guess I was self-absorbed at a young age, because I would always ask my sisters and cousins to take pictures of me. I liked to dress up and put different outfits together, and then have my sister take a picture, which I would save as a reference for that outfit idea.

One day, I met a man named Carlos Miele. He was a Brazilian designer, and he invited me to a fashion show. I wasn't sure at first because I didn't know what I'd be doing there other than to look at lovely creations I couldn't afford. But then I remembered how often I asked my sisters to take pictures of me in my mix-and-match outfits and how much fun it was to create what I thought were almost works of art (not really, but it was fun).

I met many of Carlos' friends at the show, which was just what I expected. While we were there, he surprised me by asking if I would model his clothes at his show during Olympic Fashion Week, which is the biggest week of the year for designers. I was shocked. My first thought was, *Most runway models are five-foot-eleven. I didn't fit that stereotype whatsoever and I wasn't stick skinny.* However, he kept insisting I was the perfect fit for his designs.

I asked him if I could think about it for a couple of days. He agreed to let me do so but before I got home that day, I was already beyond excited about doing it.

Two weeks later, I was in the show. I wore six outfits that fit me like a glove. I had great fun strutting and smiling for all the flashbulbs. I felt like a star, like someone really important, and I loved Carlos's clothes.

During that show, as in most, there were a ton of talent scouts in attendance. Just like in major league sports, people scout the shows looking for fresh new talent. The burnout rate is really high. What with age, fatigue, keeping your figure, travel, etc., there's always a need for new girls—the more unique, the better.

As I began to observe the workings of the shows, the designers' mindsets, the models, and the audiences, it seemed to me that no matter how pretty and professional the current models were, the scouts (or the "industry") were always looking for something unique and different—Twiggy comes to mind immediately—more exotic faces, taller, shorter, skinnier, different hair.

The agency that scouted me was Thompsons. Their rep said, "We love your look. Why don't you come in for a talk and an open call."

I didn't know what an "open call" was, but it all sounded very exciting, not that I was planning on quitting my sales job at Diesel. At this point, it was just curiosity and a lark but when I got home, I almost had a minor panic attack.

Oh God! What have I gotten myself into now?

I knew I would go but there were two potential roadblocks—Tony and my classes. If Tony knew, he'd go ballistic. There was just no way he would let me model dresses. I knew I couldn't even model fur coats. Anything that would put me up in front of a potential crowd of leering men or cameras would be a sentence to punishment.

What would I wear to this "open call" thing? I just decided to wing it. I put on one of my best outfits, did all my makeup, and went to my psychology class still only fifty-fifty on whether I'd go or not. I was still debating when I finally decided, while walking to English class, that I was going.

Arriving at the agency in a cab 40 minutes later, I went into the bathroom downstairs, re-did some of my makeup, smoothed out my tight skirt, fluffed my blouse and hair, and got in the elevator of one of those very tall and imposing buildings in Manhattan.

After waiting a few moments in an outer lobby, I was escorted into a large room, which was practically empty with the exception of five chairs. Two women and a man I didn't know, of course, sat at one end and asked me immediately to just walk around a bit. I walked over to the window, paused, turned, walked toward them, and then pulled up the lone chair about ten feet away from them.

The three kibitzed and whispered to each other, making some hand gestures, and then they turned and began to address me.

One of the women, a tall blonde, stood up and said in a serious, but almost playful way, "Suelyn. We love your look! Just love it." Then she sat down.

They talked to each other again and then the questions started: "Have you ever modeled? Where are you from? How old are you? Do you have a book?" (Meaning a portfolio of pictures.)

I knew I would have to fake it but I wasn't even sure I knew what I was doing, or what any of this might entail.

I answered all their questions and saved the "book" for last, saying, "Well, I haven't done a lot of work yet. I'm just kind of beginning. I have some good pictures, but my photographer still has them. I can get them next week," I blatantly lied. I had no photographer and hence no pictures with the exception of the ones my sisters had taken, and those weren't going to fly.

"Oh, that's fine, darling. Why don't we set up an appointment for you to come in late next week with your *book*. We'd love to take a look."

And that's how it all started. A fluke? Karma? Mistake? Call it what you will; I'd gotten over the first hurdles of a race I hadn't even been sure I was going to enter.

All the way home, I ran the gamut of emotions, from elation to guilt to *what were you thinking*? By the time I got to the apartment, and before Tony got home, I'd formed a plan. That guy Brian had said if I ever wanted to do some photos . . .

So, I began to look through my secret stash of things, found his card, and called him. That was how our relationship started. Brian turned out to be this face in the crowd, who just happened to notice me and who, on parade day, approached me . . . and the rest is history.

"Brian. Hi, this is Suelyn."

Silence.

"Suelyn who?"

"Oh, I'm sorry. How presumptuous of me. I'm the girl you met in Times Square last week. The dark-haired one. You said if I ever wanted to do some pictures to call you."

"Oh. Oh yeah. How are you?"

"Great. I have a chance to do some work for Thompsons. I've never modeled before and they've asked for my book. Could you help me?"

"Wow! That's great; Thompsons. You don't waste any time, do you. darlin'?"

"Can you do it?"

"Yes. Yes, of course. But it will have to be this week. I'm booked for the next two weeks after that."

"Perfect!"

"What and where would you like to shoot?"

"I don't know. I hadn't thought about it; any ideas?"

"How about some natural-light stuff? That would be the most flattering for now—you know, outdoors, not a lot of spots."

I didn't know what "spots" were. I thought he was talking about places outside in Manhattan.

"Yes. Yes. Can we do it this Friday? You pick the spot."

"Sure. No problem. How about the lake at the Park early in the morning? Light's better then, lots of lavenders, the perfect complement to your skin and your coloring. Let's say ten a.m."

"I'll meet you on the bridge," I said. "And thank you. Thank you so much."

I didn't know it then, but Brian was fairly new to the profession as well. He mostly did outdoor things, which is maybe why he chose the Park. Today, however, he is one of the top paparazzi photographers in the world.

On Friday, I got up before the sun and packed some nice outfits (I didn't have a clue what to take), a small makeup bag, and got on the train at 6 a.m. to go to my early class. It was going to be tight, but I knew I could make it. I didn't want to miss another class.

I had a school pass on the Metro but you can only use it twice a day and my early trip used the first swipe. After class, I took the train home and picked up my little suitcase and makeup case.

Before I left, I realized I'd already used my Metro card twice. I started to panic but then remembered Tony had purchased one of those senior discount Metro cards for his father when he'd visited. I could use that. After all, you just swipe it through the turnstile; no one is checking.

Bags in hand, I walked to the subway, went down the stairs, pulled the card out of my wallet, and swiped it through the counter. Before I could get through the turnstile, a Metro cop appeared as if I'd just robbed a jewelry store. A red light started turning overhead and I'm surprised a siren didn't come on. *Alert! Alert! Senior faker.*

"Okay, *young* lady," he said with the emphasis on young. "What are you doing using a senior pass?"

Geeze. No. Not today!

"Oh, that's my boyfriend's father's card," I quickly said. "I must've picked it up instead of my student pass." I waited.

"You realize, of course, that you're not supposed to use this. It's illegal," he admonished with the same intensity I figured he used with an illegal alien.

Time was of the essence. I didn't want Brian to think I was a flake but I had to feign guilt and remorse as the cop actually wrote me a ticket.

With all that, I still made it on time and the shoot was a huge success, or so Brian said. I wouldn't see the pictures for a few days, but the light did seem just right before the sun got too high, and I had a lot of fun prancing around, posing just like I had so many times before for my sisters and cousins.

Brian selected the best of the best and printed them for me.

"Suelyn, bring your book over and we'll put them in it."

"Uh, I can't. My book is still at Thompsons. Maybe we can buy another one together," I said, still faking everything.

"Sure. Come over. We'll go to a store I use and pick one out," he offered.

Because Brian helped me that afternoon, I was ready to present my book to the agency. In fact, Brian was a godsend. He'd not only taken great pictures, but he wouldn't accept any money from me for them. I did, however, pay for the book and off I went the next day to Thompsons.

I sat at the end of a long table while several of the agency people looked through the book, smiling, pointing, and whispering. When they were finished, one of the women said, "We would like to start submitting you for some assignments."

"Okay. I guess you'll just call me then?" I asked.

"Yes, absolutely. Stay close to your phone."

Within a few days, I'd gotten my first call. The Thompson woman said it was for a lingerie catalog for which they wanted someone with a "Latin look."

The agency sent me to a casting where I tried on the lingerie. The clients were Japanese from London. Their company was called, Tam Tam

(Princess Tam Tam).

The clothes fit like they'd been custom tailored just for me. One of the owners said, "Where did you get this body? How could you be so slim and yet have this butt? What do they put in the water in Brazil?" he asked as he circled me, his hands spinning around in the air.

He was funny and honest, and I was having fun. I was hired and modeled about 50 outfits during an all-day shoot. They were happy and I was happy. I got $3,200 for what I considered to be a fun afternoon, not unlike the ones I used to spend with my sisters and cousins for free. I almost fainted when I got the check from Thompsons. However, I had missed the day's classes at the college, which bothered me. Seems there's seldom a time when there isn't a levy to pay for happiness.

ONE DAY, I TOLD Tony I felt I needed a break, to be by myself. He came unglued. It was around 9:00 p.m. when he came over to our house. I was sitting with my mother and sisters in the living room, watching a movie when someone suddenly began banging hard on the front door. I got up to answer it, peeking carefully through the peephole first to see who it was. It was Tony.

As soon as I opened the door, he pushed it the rest of the way. I could see that he was distraught.

"I have to talk to you . . . now!" he said.

My mother and sisters realized immediately that something was wrong.

Motioning to the television, he said, "Don't stop the movie, Mrs. Medeiros. I just need to talk to your daughter."

With that, he stomped off into the kitchen, flicking his finger at me to follow. Pinning me against the counter, his breath inches from my face, he said, "I love you. Why are you ignoring my calls and messages?"

I took a deep breath, knowing I had to tell him the truth, but also bracing myself for what he might do.

"Tony, I told you; I need some space. I'm still young and I'm starting college next week. I want to hang out with my friends and cousins before I have to start studying."

He didn't respond verbally, but his expression showed nothing but total frustration and anger.

"Tony, I want to finish the movie. Come into the living room and sit with us. Everything will work out. You don't need to be angry."

I dipped under his arms, walked away, and sat back down on the couch and waited. Within a few seconds, I could hear his footsteps coming into the living room. He walked around in front of the coffee table, between us and the TV, and then from behind his back he pulled out a steak knife he'd gotten out of the kitchen drawer.

"Without you, Suelyn, there is no reason to live," he said, holding the knife against his wrist.

My mother and sisters gasped and instinctively pulled themselves into defensive balls, their legs clutched up to their chests with their arms holding onto their knees. They were huddled on the couch in disbelief, their eyes as big as teacup saucers.

There was a moment of silence and then Tony quickly pulled the knife across his right wrist. Instantly, blood began to squirt out and all over the rug and table.

Tony stood still, his face expressionless, hand and knife at his side, his skin ashen in color—no words, no movement until the knife hit the floor and he ran out the door.

My first thought was to run after him. Knowing he'd need stitches—and concerned about what else he might try to do—I quickly called his mother instead and told her what had just happened.

"Don't leave. I'll be right there," she said.

Within minutes, she drove up in front and came into our apartment.

"Oh my God," she said, looking at all the blood. "You weren't lying," which, under the circumstances, I thought was a stupid thing for her to say. *Of course I wasn't lying! What? Did she think I'd call her with such a story as some kind of a sick joke?*

Hugging me, she said, "Suelyn, you must know how much Tony loves you. I've never seen him love another girl the way he does you. Please give him another chance. You're driving him crazy."

I'm *driving* him *crazy?*

When he called me the next day, I foolishly told him I wasn't trying to break up—I just needed some space. In other words, I was too timid, worried, and frightened to call it quits like I should have, which was a huge disservice to us both.

@ ^^ # ^^ *&%* (**@-~-@ ##^^^##@9 *)__++
##@^^^%%%6 **^^—) 00 {{{# @@!!.

Later, as I continued to write my stories down, and my threads of experiences with this man began to form a quilt, I saw at the age of 18 that knowingly or not, just like the Pastor in the church, some men have a game plan when it comes to the women in their lives.

First, there are all the pleasantries, even before the wooing begins. Everything is made to appear benign, friendly, and charming. *I just want to be your friend.* Then comes the protection clause in the unspoken agreement—then the light jealousy followed by the ferocious off-the-charts jealousy. Then, sometimes comes the violence; and then the cork blows out of the bottle.

I call this entire movie "How to Boil a Frog." Here's how it works: If you put a frog in a boiling pot of water, it will just jump out—ouch! Too hot. If you want frog legs for dinner, you have to be smarter than the frog, sooooo, you put tap water in the pot and then put the frog in; the frog likes the water because it's comfortable and at room temperature. Then, ever so slowly, you turn the flame up slightly, just slightly, and soon the frog is doing the breaststroke in the water, feeling as if he's in a spa.

With each turn of the gas knob, the water becomes hotter and hotter until the frog is almost lulled to sleep and then *boom*! He's boiled, and he doesn't even know it because he's dead.

That's how you boil a frog. And that's how Tony worked his game. That's how a lot of men work their games. Now, don't get me wrong: As I said, when I fall in love, I *really* fall totally.

My acting friend (the one I lusted after), Douglas, was in London on this shoot as well. When he saw my cast, he grabbed a ballpoint pen and said, "Here, let me be the first to sign it." As he scrawled something on it, I couldn't help but thinking of furious Tony in Venice, running around like a chicken without a head. *Where has she gone? How did she sneak out? I'll kill her when I find her.* "The sky is falling," said Chicken Little.

I wouldn't tell him where I was but, still thinking foremost about my family, I sent him an email: "Hey Tony, I would've called but you broke my phone. Remember? I'm in France doing a shoot, then on to Zurich for a flight back to New York. *Ciao*. (PS: My arm is feeling much better.)"

Meanwhile, Douglas was doing everything in his power to seduce me and now more than before, I wanted to just let go and allow him to do it. Finally, I decided to tell him I had to go.

"Don't go, *mi amore*. Come to Italy with me," he said.

"No, I can't."

He grabbed me, pulled me to him, and gave me the most passionate, incredible kiss I'd ever experienced; and, like in the movies, the lights were crackling above. It was one of those, "He stole it, but then I let him have it" kisses, and it was pure heaven!

Then I came back to earth, pulled away, looked into his droopy, puppy dog eyes, and said, "I can't do this. I'll see you in New York."

Thank God, Tony wasn't on the prepaid Zurich flight so I didn't have to spend nine hours sitting next to him. However, when we touched down and entered the terminal, he was waiting for me like a jerk, holding a handful of flowers, a big smile on his face.

"Baby, I can't believe you actually went off all by yourself to France. How is your arm, sweetie?"

"I'll tell you in the taxi," I hissed. "Stop it, Tony! You're embarrassing me!"

He surprised me but, if I was a good director and had memorized the script, I shouldn't have been. I thought he'd be furious, but by now, I knew he was on a constant "mood roller coaster." Now, he was on his extra nice behavior.

Several days later, it was Fashion Week in New York. I was going to book as many shows as I could. There was no stopping me. When I told Tony I'd be busy every day and night of the week, he just said, "Okay, baby, no problem."

Later that week, I had the cast taken off my arm. According to the Venetian doctor, I wasn't supposed to, but I did anyhow. I attended one of the shows with Brian. The Mark Jacobs show was the biggest one of all and I had to attend. Brian could get in anywhere.

I WAS STILL IN COLLEGE when we went on that Hawaiian debacle for Valentine's Day. I'd decided I wanted to major in psychology. I seemed to have a very strong intuition about people, the way they thought, what motivated them, and I wanted to immerse myself in the study of the mind.

Tony was really my first "relationship," and he was a study unto himself. I didn't understand him at all, why he was the way he was, which led me to actually blame myself, But, then again, that was like an out-of-body experience, my ethereal twins each thinking differently—I'm to blame—he's crazy. I could see the evil with one eye and his acts with the other as just a normal reaction to my mistakes. I felt like the pushme-pullyou character in the *Dr. Doolittle* movie.

I wanted a degree, but more importantly, if nothing else, I wanted knowledge to understand myself fully. I'd always been the type who felt she had to learn something every day and to be productive in some way. Sure, I liked to have fun as much as anyone; when I played, I played hard (minus the drugs and very little alcohol—yes, it is possible to have fun without them)—but my underlying desire, the thing that really satisfied me and made me feel good, was learning and applying that knowledge.

At the time, I was also living with Tony in an apartment in Queens not too far from my mother.

In many of my studies, I found myself applying this knowledge of psychology to my own relationship. I would read and do the homework. If the content was appropriate to my situation, I looked at Tony through that prism, all the while subconsciously thinking that if I could figure him out, I might be able to fix him. Truth is, you can't change people, particularly a woman trying to change a man. You shouldn't try to fix them, but I wouldn't learn that until later.

I knew Tony had been a middle child who was bullied constantly by his older brother. He didn't share much about his childhood but sometimes little clues would come out and I'd take mental notes. His father used to beat him and his brothers. His older brother was always better than he was at everything. Tony never got credit from his parents. However, he would prove them wrong and become a successful stockbroker. And, by beating on me, he would show his older brother that he wasn't a wimp. That way, he got to be the bully and someone else the victim like he'd always been. For the first time in his life, he had what he thought was real power.

I loved my studies. I could feel my brain growing, getting smarter. I wasn't just adding facts, I was beginning to understand the world around me—and I began to know myself more and how to control *me*.

By nature, I'd always been one to turn negatives into positives. I learned how to block things out and not dwell on unconstructive things. I was young, but life was still too short. I promised Tony would never get one more tear from me, regardless of how hard he tried or what he did. *No* tears. *No* fears. Not a good basis for a relationship, but that had never really been my mission. My self-imposed assignment was to find a career, be successful, and find peace of mind and understanding so strong that nothing could hurt me if I didn't let it.

That was also the best contribution I could make to the well-being of my family, which made me very happy.

I LIKE TO COOK AND am very traditional, getting the "old ways" from my grandparents, So, oftentimes, I would cook dinner for Tony and me after school. However, that night, after nine hours of shooting, was different. When I got home, I told Tony, "There is something I need to talk to you about." (Men hate hearing that sentence or variations of it.)

He was sitting on the couch, so I joined him, seeing the concern on his face immediately.

"Tony, I think I want to do some modeling," was the simplest, most direct, and honest thing I could say.

"What? What are you talking about?" (You can almost hear his voice and see his face, can't you?) Why would you want to be a model?"

"I'm not sure. I was just thinking about it," I said, beginning to backpedal already.

"That's ridiculous. You're going to school and now you want to model?"

"Yes," I answered, regaining my footing.

"No. You are *not* going to model. That's not for you." (Funny how so many men in our lives think they know what's best for us.) "That's *definitely* not for you," he insisted. "Most models start when they're about thirteen, super skinny, and six feet tall."

Not to be deterred, I retorted, "Yeah. Well. There are other types of models and other *things* to model than just slinky dresses. I know I can do this."

Of course, I didn't tell him I'd spent the day doing just that—lingerie, no less.

"Listen. I don't know where this is coming from, but you get that idea out of your head. You are *not* going to model. I don't like it and your parents won't like it when I tell them. And that's final."

I didn't answer—just smiled knowingly and walked into the kitchen to prepare dinner. Despite Tony's attitude and bullying, I was in a great mood. I knew that his mention of my parents was a threat meant to bolster his position, but it didn't matter. I was so determined and focused on this new career that I didn't care.

I began seriously modeling that very week. I didn't tell Tony. I hid the jobs and started my own bank account. The calls began coming in regularly, and I got booked for my first magazine within two weeks. The shoot was for QT bras. It was a picture of me lying across a bed with a super coverage, super ugly bra. That was my first taste of magazines. Later, when it came out, I was given a copy by the agency but was afraid to take it home. I asked the woman at the agency if she would keep it there in a file for me. *Maybe she can begin to keep an ongoing file of my work,* I thought.

I lied and told her I was moving and didn't want it to get lost. So far, I'd been doing a lot of lying. I lied to the first agency people about my book. I also lied to Brian about my book. I lied to Tony about my work. I lied to the train cop, and now I was lying to the agency woman again. I guess you can call those "white lies." I was beginning to learn, though, what the phrase, "Fake it till you make it," meant.

To me, it meant that if I wanted something, if I had a passion for it, then sometimes I might have to fake it to take advantage of an opportunity. The other thing I learned was the power of that overused word, "passion." It's not something I could go look for or invent. Passion was something I felt from the inside out, and I was smart enough to know that if I could make money, real good money doing something I loved, then everything was right in the world for me—almost everything. There is always an admittance fee and, in my case, that was Tony.

During this time, I was getting numerous jobs, hiding them all, and still going to school. Brian and I were becoming great friends and we did two other shoots together, one on a street in Manhattan with the Empire State Building in the background. Mostly, though, I would just put on an outfit, he'd grab his Nikon, and we'd go outdoors and just shoot. Most of the shots came out fantastic. He was and is a phenomenal photographer. He was a beginner like me, with a lot of talent and a passion to have fun with it and succeed.

I first introduced Brian to my family and then tried to figure out a way to introduce him to Tony. Looking back now, off the subject a little, I can see how hard I was trying to live a "normal" life with an abnormal man—how hard I tried to pretend that all his abuse was almost normal, what many women must have been putting up with just to have an anchor, security. *Ugh!*

At any rate, I told him I wanted him to meet Brian, that he was a photographer, and I wanted to do some pictures for myself and for us (Tony and me).

"Oh no. Is this the modeling thing again?" were the first words out of Tony's mouth.

"No. I know this photographer who is really funny. He's so gay, you'll get a kick out of him," I said, regretting the words before they reached Tony's ears. What did his sexual perspective have on anything? I was just trying to soften up my prey a little bit.

Tony was a tough Italian and very homophobic, but I figured that would deter his anger since Brian would not be a threat.

"Where did you meet this guy?"

I lied once again. "I met him doing a project at school, some photography stuff, and I took his card. At the time, I was thinking of a photographer for my cousin's wedding," (which seemed plausible). "And another thing," I added for ammunition, "we didn't know what we were going to get her for her wedding. Getting the photographer and all the pictures would be fantastic!" I said enthusiastically, suddenly realizing it was a damned good idea to boot. *Kill two birds with one stone.*

I waited for Tony's response. Waited some more. Waited still more until he finally said, "Oh, okay. Brian is your new gay friend."

Psychologically speaking, Tony had just given me a Black American Express card with an unlimited budget. I would now be able to shoot to my heart's content.

CHAPTER FOUR

Set-up to a Sad Story

TIME PASSED; I CONTINUED modeling and going to school. I'd been studying at Hunter college for 18 months when I met who I thought was my first true love, (even though I was still living with Tony.) Of course, there had been boyfriends, mentors, and others, but at that time, I thought Douglas was "it."

We met on the set of an ad campaign for a Brazilian energy beverage, Flash Power Energy Drink, which was just becoming known and popular in Europe. I was given the part of the "Campaign Girl," the visual identity, and Douglas was selected to be the "Campaign Guy."

He was half-Brazilian and half-Italian, born and raised in Brazil. He could have passed for my brother, but thank God, he wasn't. Douglas was six-foot-one, bronze skin, silky long dark hair, and bright hazel eyes, who possessed a bad-boy image, not altogether undeserved.

Douglas had begun his acting career in Brazil in the TV soaps and made a name for himself there. In his early 20s, he moved to Italy to model for D&G and to bond with his father. Now he was in New York working various gigs.

One look at him and I knew I had to stay away.

The energy drink shoot was scheduled for four hours prior, for which he spent most of his time primping and asking the makeup girl to powder his sweaty forehead or touch up his cheeks.

I kept thinking, *steer clear and, oh boy, get over yourself. You don't even need makeup.* The other part of me, the part I abhorred, kept saying, *I would love to jump on you and make passionate love.* The way he flicked his hair, the way he chewed his gum, he just had an aura of "I'm too cool for school" about him. I was drawn to and repelled by him, both at the same time, mostly drawn like a moth to a flame who knows the light is bright and hot, but who keeps hanging around anyhow.

He made me woozy, so I knew I had to finish the shoot and be gone because I couldn't trust myself.

A few weeks later, I was booked for a film part, the love interest in a Mafia movie—*My Brother's Keeper*—that included Douglas in a small part. My (character's) boyfriend was one of the Mafia bosses who was Albanian and I was secretly assigned to kill him.

For three weeks, Douglas was a professional. Even so, during breaks, I would run from him and hide in my makeup room. He would always find me, like a cat intent on one particular mouse. He would come around, always jovial, cracking jokes, and making fun of other people on the set in Portuguese, a language only the two of us spoke.

When I'd booked the movie, I was still in school so in order to take the job, I had to lock my credits for that semester. My career was really beginning to take off and I was booking jobs almost every day from fashion, to magazines, videos, and what I called "prop girls," those who are hired to smile, hang around and look sexy, and not talk.

I'd had my second cover on magazines by this point and a few on the way. Douglas was very funny and entertaining but I still kept a safe distance. He would tease me and say, "So Sue, when are you going to take me out?" to which I would respond, "My name is Suelyn, not Sue."

Aside from his physical threats, Tony always had a million other ploys or new tactics to help ensure that I would stick around. Whenever he was cruel, he'd come up with something to distract me from his pathology. This time, he told me he had a plan to bring my father back into the country—illegally, of course. For $10,000, he'd met a guy who could bring my father across the Mexican border.

I was supposed to fall for the fact that he was going to pay that much money to make me happy; that he wanted me to be with my entire family; that he wanted to "build a family" with me; and that I shouldn't let Hollywood get to my head—it and my heart should be there with him and my family. I didn't fall for it, but I did want to see my father again. Tony set the wheels in motion so that I was once again "beholdin'" to him, at least until my father was safely in the country.

I told him I thought it was too risky. "Tony, if he gets caught, they'll send him to prison for life."

"It doesn't work like that. If he's here, he could work under a different name. At least your family will be here," Tony said, and I immediately realized that this was, in fact, just another one of his ploys. Not only was it to make him look good, but it was also to ensure that I didn't go back to my family because he could bring everyone to me.

After a great deal of thought between my parents and me, and taking into account the risks, we decided to bring Dad across the border. He flew to Columbia first and from there into Mexico. Tony had already paid the smuggler the deposit.

When my father got into Mexico, he had no money—none. He was unable to call us. Four days passed without word. We were worried to death. I wanted to kill Tony as I yelled, "I told you so!" at him.

Later, after my father made it to the States, he told us the horrific story of what had happened. He'd found the smuggler, taken a boat with some other people, and trudged through some pretty dense forest before breaking his foot. At that point, he managed somehow to call us; but not wanting us to worry, he just said that there was going to be a small delay, just for a few more days.

I blamed myself for the entire thing. It was a disaster, and I caused my family so much pain. Of course, we didn't know that the smuggler abandoned him in the jungle when he broke his foot. He spent the next two days hobbling through the forest, not knowing where he was, until a farmer found and helped him. Eventually, days later, he was able to contact us from the border outside San Diego.

Tony and I boarded the next plane, got a hotel room, and then drove to Tijuana the next morning. Tony got Dad through Customs somehow, but the smuggler was not there and so Tony did not have to pay the balance. We flew back to New York the next day, my father using an ID that Tony had obtained for him.

Once we were back in New York, Tony offered to help my father. He wanted to finance him so that he could start his own construction company. Now, Tony was doing stock deals as well as investing in my father's firm.

All of that was good and I was so glad to have my father back, but I knew I was truly stuck. Now my father and Tony were business partners; Tony had accomplished what he said he would and I knew I now owed a debt too big to flee.

A couple of weeks later, it was time for Fashion Week again. I went and afterward did some photos for a double *XL Magazine* issue, and was invited to the Marc Jacobs' fashion show by a friend who was in Jacobs' entourage.

As fate would have it, there were a lot of celebrities there and among them was Fifty Cent, the rapper. I had never met him and did not talk to him during the show, but afterwards when we were leaving, as we stood in line to get out the door, unbeknownst to me, a *New York Post* photographer took our picture. I was stuck behind some people and Fifty Cent was standing behind me.

That night I was home with Tony. We were in the living room watching television. He seemed quiet and content and I fixed us a snack. When I brought it back and sat on the couch, he got up and went into the bedroom. I continued to watch the program and munch on the cheese and apples when I suddenly felt the cold hard edge of something on the back of my neck. I couldn't imagine what it might be, so I slowly turned to see Tony with a .45 automatic pistol now touching the temple on my head.

I knew he had a gun, the one he'd told me he kept in case anyone ever broke in, the one he kept to protect me—the one that was now ironically aimed at me. Not moving a muscle, I froze and caught my breath. My heart was about to pound through my chest. He hadn't said a word, but I could see "that look" on his face.

"Tony, what are you doing? Is this some kind of sick joke?"

He didn't answer. Not having a clue what to do or how to act to diffuse him, I turned my head back toward the television, when I heard the gun cock, and I almost peed my pants.

After what seemed an eternity, he said, "Are you going to tell me the truth now?"

"What are you talking about, Tony? Why are you doing this?" My school studies in psychology started to kick in. *Keep him calm. Don't panic.*

He threw a copy of the *New York Post* in my lap.

"First of all, tell me the truth. Answer yes or no," he said. He didn't need to explain any further. I slowly looked down at the newspaper and there about six inches tall was a picture of what appeared to be Fifty Cent and me leaving the show together.

"If this is going to be our last day, I need to know the truth," Tony said. "You can change your destiny right now if you just tell me the truth. How long have you been fucking him?" he screamed.

I could see he was past the boiling point.

"Tony, you don't know what you're saying. I don't know what you've heard or what anyone has told you, but I wasn't with that man. We were just leaving the fashion show at the same time."

I could see he was getting angrier and much more nervous, so I tried to change my approach, when he said, "I will shoot you and then I will shoot myself. We will go out together and then, maybe then, we can truly be together forever."

Now I knew I was in real trouble. He'd obviously gone off the deep end.

"Listen, Tony. Can you please calm down? We were both at the event, but not together. There were a lot of people there, including a lot of rappers. They like their expensive designer clothes," I tried to explain. "I didn't even know he was standing behind me. I don't know the man. I am not cheating on you."

Slowly, he put the gun down on a chair and I finally took a much-needed breath.

"Why don't you give me the gun so we can talk, Tony?"

Then he started babbling about taking his own life, life wasn't worth anything without me, and he was going to end it right now.

———⟨⟩———

FOR SO MANY REASONS, it was an odd time in my life, mostly because of Tony. He'd confided in me earlier that his older brother had been in jail on drug charges for quite some time. He was a dealer who brought drugs in from the Dominican Republic, and he was about to be released.

I ended up confiding in him that my father was also in jail. In time, I would go with Tony to visit his brother in prison and then Tony would reciprocate and come with me to visit my father in prison. It was all very weird, but it got weirder.

I thought Tony's brother looked like a thug in prison, but I gave him the benefit of the doubt because of his outfit and his circumstances when we visited. However, when he got out, he still looked like a thug. He was covered with tattoos, dressed in sloppy jeans and T-shirts and, in general, was just the opposite of his brother in the way he dressed and acted. He smoked incessantly and, of course, did drugs (two things Tony never did).

It didn't take long for Tony's brother's influence to become a part of Tony's life and by extension, mine. We were still in Queens when his brother convinced Tony to go in with him on some big deal, to which I wasn't privy.

One day I was home, cooking in the kitchen. I opened the oven, which I never used, to find a pan. Inside were four huge bags of weed. I was stunned! *How could I not know?* I didn't like his brother or what he stood for, and I didn't know what either of them had been up to. At that point, I decided to search the rest of the house, thinking the horrible thought that my discovery in the oven might be just the tip of the iceberg—and it was.

In the closet were more bags of weed hidden in Tony's shoeboxes. *How did I not know about all this?*

I confronted Tony as soon as he walked in the door that night. He was in a quiet mood when I held out one of the bags. "What the hell is going on?" I said, holding the box three inches from his face. "I'm not going to be a part of this! What's going on? How long has this been going on?" I was furious.

Tony tried to convince me that he was just holding it all for his brother, that he had nothing to do with the sales. "I'm not involved with anything," he said.

"Yes, you are. You're hiding his drugs in *our* home. You can't get more involved than that," I yelled, now pacing the living room.

The final straw was his reply, "You're a woman. You have no say."

"That's your answer?" I said, in his face again. "*That's* your answer?"

I knew it was fruitless. He was going to act the tough guy, the big man, and if he couldn't lie his way out of it, he would just pull the macho thing on me. I slept on the couch that night, for all of about an hour. My heart just wouldn't stop its excessive pounding all night.

The next morning, I tried to avoid him, but it was difficult in the small apartment. Finally, we clashed in the kitchen.

"Suelyn, listen. My brother's been away for a long time. He needs help in getting started again. He doesn't have a home and he has no money. He's my brother, for God's sake."

"Brother or not, I'm not going to be a part of this."

"I'm just keeping it for him. That's the truth."

Not only was I now caught in his web, living the life of a married adult, but I was really only a teenager. That's when I realized that my modeling career was going to be my ticket out, away from this man.

IT WAS FEBRUARY 12, 2004. I was anticipating Valentine's Day (as most girls do and most men don't); however, I was very pleasantly surprised when Tony announced that he was taking me to Hawaii. Visions of warm weather, balmy blue seas, and palm trees swaying quickly replaced the view out of our Queens apartment—cold gray and dull.

Tony was doing well as a broker. The stock market was alive with activity and so he was in a good mood. We flew first class and landed in Waikiki on a Friday, also Valentine's Day, and were greeted as everyone was upon arrival, with dancing women wearing coconut halves as bikini tops; their grass skirts swaying in the breeze. We each received a lei around our necks and a big, *Aloha*.

I was smiling when we arrived in our room, to find another greeting waiting—rose petals everywhere! On the bed, the red and pink petals formed a heart shape, and on the bed stand next to the bed was a bottle of champagne in a silver bucket of ice along with six of the biggest chocolate-covered strawberries I'd ever seen; they were the size of very large apricots!

Tony had already planned our adventures, beginning with the very next morning's scuba diving lessons in the hotel pool. On the following day, we were taken out to the ocean where we continued to learn to adjust to the much deeper water.

To some people, the depth and the pressure are problems for their ears, but not for me. I was taking to the whole experience like a newborn fish, all in preparation for our shark dive the next day.

The instructor was a handsome young man in his 20s; which meant that Tony immediately didn't like him. First, the instructor helped us to slide down a rope into the warm water, explaining that we would go slow to see how we adjusted to the change in depth, a little at a time. I was fine at each three—or four-foot dive. However, I could tell Tony wasn't doing as well because his ears weren't popping.

As I reached the ocean floor, I couldn't find Tony. He'd disappeared. When I looked up, I could see that he and the instructor were slowly ascending. The instructor was pointing to his ears, telling me that Tony was having problems with the depth. They returned to the boat while I just continued to enjoy the fascinating and astounding fish that continued to swim around me, without a care in the world, as if I was just another new fish—and I almost felt that way, almost like a mermaid.

The morning of the shark dive, I was so excited I couldn't eat breakfast. I just wanted to get to the docks.

Just like in the movies, the day and the scenery were exactly as I'd pictured they'd be. The captain got us all settled in for the long ride out to deeper waters; in particular, he said, an area where Great Whites frequently ate.

About 20 minutes later, the captain shut off the engines and dropped anchor. After a brief speech by the same instructor about safety and how the cages worked, our cage was readied.

Tony and I were helped into the cage by the instructor, which was then slowly lowered into the water.

"Keep your hands inside the cage," were the last words I heard the young instructor yell out.

As the cage descended lower and lower, Tony moved further and further away from the bars to the middle of the cage. I was thrilled and unfazed as I stood, my body and hands touching the metal bars.

Dead fish suddenly started floating down from above. The water was so pure we could clearly see the bottom of the boat. One of the deckhands was "chumming" (as they called it), or tossing bait in to attract the Whites.

It seemed only seconds before they started to arrive. Enormous, fierce beasts with surprisingly small beady eyes began thrashing in the water around us. To me, they were beautiful creatures: powerful, fearless, and yet sleek and handsome.

However, Tony felt differently. He stood as rigid as a bronze statue in the middle of the cage, his eyes constantly darting side to side as if one of the sharks was going to sneak up on him and somehow get into the cage.

Meanwhile, I was putting my arm all the way through the bars and patting the sharks on their backs as they slid by, eyeing us inquisitively—undoubtedly as food. The more chum that came down, the more excited the sharks became. Then, when they started banging their huge bodies against the cage, I thought Tony was going to pass out. However, we were still at a depth he could tolerate so as he froze, I continued to stroke the sharks.

When we were pulled up and got back into the boat, the instructor came over and congratulated us, complimenting me by saying that I was a natural. Tony was silent—not out of fear any longer, but because he was angry. I knew instinctively from the expression on his face I'd come to know so well, that he was jealous and resentful of the instructor's attention.

Tony was silent and brooding all the way back to the hotel. He opened the door and walked in ahead of me, almost slamming the door in my face.

The minute I was in the room, my wonderful fairy tale day was over. I was certainly no longer a mermaid. I was about to become a punching bag. As I put my bag on the bed, Tony whirled around and punched me in the face. No matter how jealous he had been in the past, he'd never touched me and, yet, here I was now, lying on the floor, blood pouring out of my nose, my head spinning. Although I really shouldn't have been, I was stunned nonetheless.

"You little bitch," he screamed while I pushed myself away from him with the heels of my feet and the palms of my hands. "I can't believe I've brought you here all the way from New York and you spend the entire day flirting with that fuck on the boat—and right in front of me. You're lucky I didn't kill him!"

The veins in Tony's neck were as thick as dockworkers' ropes. His face was so red I thought his head was going to blow off. He kept pacing in circles with his fists clenched, almost like a bull about to make another run at the matador holding the red cape.

I was beyond disbelief. In fact, I think I was truly in shock.

Now, cowering by the edge of the bed, he came at me, grabbed the neck of my blouse and began slapping me.

"I wish the sharks had eaten you," he yelled.

"What do you mean? I can't believe you're this angry. I didn't flirt with him," I said, to no avail. My face was burning and I could feel my eyes swelling, the blood now running quickly down my chin all the way to my shorts.

"You fucking bitch," he kept yelling. I was crying.

Normally, I would have fought back, but not with Tony. I never could fight him. As he stood back, I thought: *Maybe I did flirt with the instructor unknowingly just by how I was dressed or the fact that I was pleasant with him—or maybe just because I smiled.*

"Tony, baby. It won't happen again," I stammered.

Oh my God, just writing those words makes me sick to my stomach. *What a fool I was. I was nothing more than a bug underfoot, an object, a sad pet dog who had disobeyed.*

When he'd backed off and retreated, fuming, to the balcony, I went into the bathroom, locked the door, got into the shower, and stayed there. Within a few minutes, he was knocking at the door. Using his best "sweet" voice, he said, "Come on, sweetie, sweet Sue-Sue. Come out and come to bed with me."

I didn't answer as I wrapped myself in a towel and wiped the mist off the mirror to see my bloated face, still hot and red with a white handprint emblazoned on my cheek.

Again, a knock came but no voice. When I finally went out, he walked over to me and I flinched violently. He grabbed me and hugged me and then picked me up and put me on the bed like a child. I clutched my arms around myself and braced against another attack. *Why wasn't I fighting back?*

Tony seemed calm now—his mood turning on and off as easily as a light switch. Of course, I'd later learn from observing so many people—their moods, reactions, and motivations—that this was a clear signal of someone who was unbalanced. Any calm or peace he'd exhibited around me had been nothing but an act. Then he slowly reached under my pillow, pulling out a small, shiny gold box with a red ribbon around it. Wearing the expression of a little boy on his face, he held the box in both hands and said, "Sweetie, I really overreacted, I admit. I love you, but imagine how you would feel if your ears popped and all that water came rushing in. It was excruciating. My ears still hurt."

The two situations didn't make sense. Jealous of another man for no reason or achy ears, which was it? I felt like two people, both removed from my physical body. For some unknown reason, one was trying to believe this man loved and cared about me, and the other was all-knowing and omniscient, recognizing without a doubt, that he was crazy.

96

Still holding the box, Tony reached out to me and said, "I'm sorry. This is your Valentine's present. Open it." He smiled as if nothing out of the ordinary had just occurred. In his mind, everything would be just peachy now that he'd given me a gift and apologized.

I didn't care about his stupid gift. I didn't care about his pitiful apology. The pain inside was far deeper than those on my face. In that second, I wanted to swipe my hand across his and knock the little box across the room. I wanted to disappear.

"Sweetie, I love you," he continued, leaning over to kiss my cheek. "I'll make it all right. Don't ruin our trip."

Huh? Don't ruin our trip? Are you insane?

I was frightened because I knew I was trapped.

Not paying any attention to my expression of horror, or that I was slowly scooting inch by inch away from him, he began to open the box himself. He laid the bow across my lap, removed the lid, and pulled out an astounding diamond, star-shaped necklace with matching diamond studs and bracelet. Smiling, he said, "You're my star."

It's difficult to sum up my feelings at that moment. I was feeling a mixture of emotions: anger, exhaustion, bewilderment, hate. I didn't throw the jewelry in the trash, but I never wore it either, which he noticed but never mentioned.

AFTER THE TRIP TO HAWAII, Tony and I did a lot of traveling to Aruba, the Bahamas, and then Europe. I had the energy drink shoot and the movie behind me, as well as Douglas. Tony thought the Europe trip would bring us closer together, but he also had other things he had to do there. We were not the only thing on his agenda.

He was also shopping around for a dog, a Rotweiller to be exact. He wanted to buy the dog and then have it trained in the finest training camp in the world, in Germany.

Our first stop was Switzerland for some banking. Then we went to Germany so Tony could put his name on a waiting list for the dog. He said he would pay extra to be bumped up to the top of the long waiting list.

After three days in Germany, it was time to go to Italy. Our first stop was Florence where Tony claimed his roots since his father's family had been from there. Then we went to Venice, which was the most magical stop for me. No cars, of course, just boats. I couldn't stop taking pictures! I was the ultimate tourist.

Everything was going well. I spent the days sightseeing, visiting the famous glass factory, riding in the boats, enjoying the art, seeing everything I could devour. Tony was being "normal." I was feeling happy and relieved that he was calm and then, as it so often does when you're feeling on top of the world, all hell broke loose. But the worst part was, I couldn't figure out why.

We were in our hotel room. Tony was working on his laptop, and I was on my phone as usual. Suddenly, he stood up, slammed his laptop screen down, and quickly walked toward me. I instantly knew something wasn't right—whatever was wrong, it was evil. He slapped the phone out of my hand and it went crashing against the brick wall, splintering into pieces.

"Why did you do that?" I asked, standing up.

As I began to collect the pieces, he grabbed my arm and began twisting it backwards.

"Tony, you're hurting me! *Stop!*"

"What the fuck is *My Brother's Keeper*, and what did you have to do with it?" he raged.

He wouldn't let go. My arm was killing me.

"It was a small movie. I had a little role in it."

Unbeknownst to me, the trailer for the movie was running by now and a friend of Tony's had copied and sent it to him.

"You fucking whore. You've been lying to me again. Who did you screw in the movie?"

"Please, Tony, no one. *Please stop,*" and as I screamed those words, he snapped my arm and then pushed me to the floor. I felt like I was going to pass out. The pain of the broken bone was almost unbearable, but I didn't want to cry and I didn't want him to know he'd hurt me.

Tony retreated to the bathroom. I struggled to get up and then dialed the front desk. "Miss, I think I've broken my arm. Could you send a doctor up to room 1053?"

"Yes. Certainly. Immediately. I will also call for an ambulance right away," she said.

I sat down on a nearby chair as Tony came out of the bathroom.

"You stupid bitch! Now look what you've made me do. *You did this to yourself,*" he shouted. He was out of control, pacing, flapping his arms, and yelling. I held my arm, walked over to the liquor table and, with one hand, opened a bottle of vodka, popped five Tylenols in my mouth, washing them down with the alcohol. Now standing by the window, within minutes, I could see and hear the ambulance pulling up in front downstairs.

A bellman knocked at the door; I answered. Tony sat. There was a nurse, a stretcher, and an EMT. I told them I could walk and then Tony tried to join the parade. I told him to stay but he didn't listen and came anyway.

Downstairs and out to the boat we all walked, the EMT on one side, the nurse on the other side, the bellman, and Tony—who was trailing behind, looking disgusted and terribly inconvenienced.

On the ambulance boat, the EMT examined my arm and asked, "How did this happen, madam?"

"I had a bad fall," and then I let out a fake laugh.

As this conversation was going on and the EMT was preparing a splint, Tony came up behind, caressing me for the cameras. I would have had my leg broken as well, just to see him fall in the water and drown right at that moment. *What a scab. What an idiot. What a freak. What a psychopath.*

We motored around other boats, but no siren was used. Within a couple of minutes, we were at a hospital emergency room. When the doctor arrived to examine me sitting on the gurney, Tony whispered something in his ear in Italian and then stuffed some money in the pocket of his white coat.

After his examination, the doctor said, "Obviously, it is broken. First, we must set it."

"Okay. Let's do it."

"This will hurt. I will have to give you some morphine," he said, putting his hand out to a nurse.

"No, no. No shots. Just do it," I replied.

The doctor looked incredulous. "It will hurt a great deal," he said.

"Are you sure?"

"Yes. Yes, just set it."

With that, I grabbed my sweater and bit down hard. The doctor put two large wooden splints on my arm, one on the top and one on the bottom and then said, "Okay, this will only hurt for a few seconds. After the bone is set, the pain will mostly go away," and then he grabbed the splints and my arm in his hands like a giant salami sandwich and squeezed quick and hard.

I saw stars. I immediately broke out in a massive sweat. They could hear me screaming all the way to the fourth floor of the building. I came very, very close to passing out and then it was over, just as the doctor had said. After all that, they put a cast on it, gave me some pain pills, and I was dismissed.

I walked out with Tony silently following me. We went back to the hotel in the ambulance boat. As it motored through the canals, I was plotting my escape. My hate for this man was higher and more furious than it had ever been before. It made me nauseous to even look at him. The handsome man I once loved—the debonair Italian—was now a mere freak: a sick, weak, disgusting slime, a mere shadow of a man.

I wouldn't even have had to return to the hotel with him. I could have just left all my clothes, everything, at the hotel; gone to the airport; bought a ticket to New York; and sat there until the plane loaded. But I couldn't. I was trapped. Tony's arrangements to have my father come into the country using the mule in Mexico were just two weeks off. It was all set to happen.

This would be the most difficult acting job of my young life and indeed, in many ways, the experience did serve me well in acting later. It gave me life experiences to draw from for emotion and, boy, there were plenty of *those* experiences brewing—so I stayed, got into character, and began to play the role of my life in my own movie.

That's when I realized that we all live in our own movies. We star in them, we direct them, and we produce them. We may think we're just victims, or life is just a series of mostly uncontrollable events that we usually can't affect, but that isn't the case.

Looking back at that moment, in particular, I knew that life, our landscape, our friends, our undertakings, and our emotions are all as we would have them. I realized then that if this was my movie and I was the star and director, I was going to change the script. But, at the time, I didn't consider what I owed or how much I should be careful.

When we got back to the hotel, Tony was all weepy and sorry—he was downright pathetic. The pain pills had taken effect and I was getting goofy, so I told him, "I'm going to lie down and take a nap."

I fell asleep on the bed instantly with him blubbering how much he was sorry, a far too familiar scene. If I had been on set directing, I would have had someone take him out back and beat him to within an inch of his life and then called a cab to take him nowhere.

The next day, he took me shopping in all the expensive stores, of course, thinking his baubles and gifts would erase the prior day. My only need then was for a new phone, but I couldn't find one that used my old SIM card, which I had managed to retrieve before he broke it, too, so we returned to the hotel room. When we got there, I told him I was going downstairs to the business center to use the computer. He said, "No need. Use mine." I argued, he relented, and I got in the elevator and went to the lobby.

I sat at one of the computers and used my new secret email, the one I used for business. Flash Power was doing a campaign in London and I was supposed to be there, but I hadn't gone because Tony would never have been okay with it; and, again, I had my father's safe arrival hanging over my head.

However, after contacting Flash, I changed my mind. I got all the information I needed online and told my agent I was going to meet the crew in London—all I had to do was take a ferry ride and then the train.

I took a deep breath, turned off the computer, and went back to the room, acting as if nothing had happened. I pretended to sleep until Tony fell into a deep snore. When I was sure he was asleep, I gingerly gathered some things and tiptoed out the door, taking a boat taxi to the ferry for the 6:00 a.m. ride.

Later that afternoon, I was safely in London where, of course, everyone wanted to know what happened to my arm. Expecting that this was going to happen, I had rehearsed a story. "I slipped off the dock in Venice, hitting my arm and breaking it against the edge of the boat before I splashed into the water."

As the story needed to be repeated often that first day, I added embellishments: "Oh yes, I hit the water with a flat thud and then swam all the way back to the dock, not even feeling the pain until I tried to climb up, out of the water."

Everyone was duly impressed.

WE LONG FOR THE old days because we tend to remember only the good parts and, of course, we were younger. I never want to go back to being 17 again. It was a bad year.

Tony and I had been seeing each other for about five months. Since I was still 17, I was also still living with my mother and sisters. One day, Tony presented me with tickets to Florida—a week of adventure at all the theme parks. He knew how much I loved the parks. He knew a lot about me. I was still a giddy kid wanting to ride the roller coasters while, at the same time, trying to grow up. When you're 17, all you want is to be 18 and an "official" adult.

It didn't take him long to get me excited: "We'll go to Universal Studios, Disney World, Sea World; all the parks," he said with a big smile. I was so excited, after school that day, I told my mother all about the trip but she, of course, came unglued.

"Absolutely not," she said. "You're not old enough."

I went anyway (of course).

We stayed at the Disney World Resort for a fun-filled week of excitement and on our last night, we went out for a special dinner.

From the other side of the crisp white cloth-covered dinner table and between two very tall elegant candles, Tony looked me in the eyes intently, cleared his throat, and said, "Suelyn, I'm in love with you. I want you to move in with me."

I nearly choked on my steak. Recovering, I didn't look directly at him as I said, "Tony, you're moving too fast. We've only been dating for six months."

"I know, but I didn't even need that much time. I love you with all my heart," he said.

"I know, Tony, but we need to slow down a little."

"Suelyn, I want to be with you forever. I want to have a family with you," he replied, not wanting to hear any rebuttal. With that, he pulled out a small box. I knew immediately what it was, but I didn't want it to be.

Don't let that be a ring. Don't *let that be a ring.*

He put the box on the table and slid it over next to my hand. "Suelyn, will you marry me?"

Oh God. Oh God.

"Tony, you're a great guy. I like you and I want to get to know you better, but this is too soon," I said, not touching the box. "I don't want to rush anything."

Tony sat back in his chair, seeming to give up the fight. He sighed, then he said, "Okay. I understand. You need some time to think. No pressure."

While I pretended to be involved with my food, I thought I was off the hook, at least temporarily

"I'll tell you what. Let's do this," he said, coming back to life. "You keep the ring. Put it in a safe place and when you feel the time is right, surprise me by just putting it on. When I see it on your finger, I'll know you're ready."

I should have never come on this trip. Now I feel guiltier than ever.

We returned to Queens the next day and when I opened the front door to my mother's apartment, she was waiting for me, ready and furious.

"Where have you been? Why didn't you call?" she yelled, pacing the living room floor. "Do you think you can leave like that without a word and then come prancing back in here like some little princess?"

She was hotter than I'd ever seen her.

"I don't want you to ever see that man again. You are too young. You're still in school. You tell him *adios* and stay here instead of living at his place ninety percent of the time. You go to school and finish your education. This kind of behavior is *not* going to fly in my house."

"Mom, I'm still going to school; and I want to live a normal life and date him."

But she was relentless. "Then pack your bags and move in with him. Go ahead, take all your stuff; you've pretty much done that already anyhow."

"You're kicking me out?" I said incredulously.

"No. You kicked yourself out," she replied and then turned and stomped off to the kitchen.

Now, my attention turned to my family and away from my childish wants. I followed her down the hall to the kitchen. "Mom, *please*. I will never see him again. I'm sorry I've hurt you."

She would have none of it, none of me. I felt lower than a snake. But here's the kicker, a 17-year-old kicker—I left that afternoon and went to Tony's, where he stood, waiting and smiling in his living room. I gave myself up. I don't even really know why.

Now what do I do? I'm stuck with Tony.

I was too full of pride to go back home and say I was wrong, so I decided I would make it work somehow.

He really loves me. How bad can it be?

(One of many mistakes made when growing up.)

CHAPTER FIVE

Moving in with Tony

THE FINANCIAL WORLD TONY had chosen was paying dividends. He was doing very well and found an apartment for us near his job on Wall Street. It was at 10 Hanover Square, a gorgeous 2,500 square foot, two-bedroom layout. The building was actually still under construction. The floor plan and view were fantastic, with just one minor flaw—since Tony had over 200 suits, our closet was far too small. I don't think he owned a pair of jeans or a single T-shirt, but he definitely had plenty of suits and dress shirts. And, of course, I had a ton of things as well—my shoe collection alone rivaled Emelda Marcos in her early years. However, Tony managed to come up with a solution: He would knock out some walls and convert the second bedroom into a giant closet.

Within the week, workers were busy creating the "dream" closet. Tony had designed it so we could enter either of the two sides, so there would essentially be two "drive-in" closets and our clothes would never have to touch.

When we moved in, Tony had his black S55 Benz that he loved, and he bought me a diamond-blue SL500 hardtop convertible. I loved that car. The only snag, which at that young age didn't seem a problem, was that his credit had taken a big hit when he was younger (another red flag) so he bought the cars under my name (along with plenty of other things). Sometimes he even used his father's name.

❖

My 20ᵗʰ Birthday

IT WAS A SURPRISE. Tony planned the whole thing at Cipriani two blocks from our Hanover Square apartment. He invited all his new broker friends who, in turn, brought all of their plastic girlfriends. Although it was *my* birthday and a few of my friends were there, it felt more like Tony's party. Additionally, it had been a sad week because my mother had been diagnosed with Lupus and we had spent considerable time seeking treatment.

The minute we arrived at Cipriani, Tony gave me a big kiss and then whispered in my ear, "Now, remember, you're turning twenty-four today. Be sure to remind your mother and friends."

After about five minutes, I could feel a strange vibe in the room. People were talking, but saying nothing. It was a room full of fake people saying boring things to make even more boring conversation. They weren't my kind of people, so I stuck close to my mother and a couple of my friends.

Standing by the window, trying to avoid everyone, I heard a clamor at the door. Turning, I saw that it was Rafael Maximilliano Verga, the Brazilian supermodel, who oddly enough had green eyes and blond hair, too. I'd met him during Fashion Week and Brian had invited him without telling me—after all, it *was* a surprise party.

The minute I saw him, my heart stopped, not because of his looks but because of the trouble I knew was inevitably going to take place. When he saw me, he came over immediately with his brother, who was just as gorgeous. Everyone in the room had stopped talking, and I suddenly felt as though 50 klieg lights were shining on me. The crowd parted as he approached and said in Portuguese, "*Feliz Anniversario* (Happy Birthday), Suelyn," and then he gave me a kiss

107

on each cheek. In Brazil, this is common, as it is in many other countries. Then, his brother followed up with the same custom.

I froze.

As we talked, my mother came over and said, "Suelyn. Aren't you going to introduce me to your friends?"

My heart started beating even faster as Tony began to approach me with "that look" on his face. I steeled myself and before he started to say something stupid, I whispered in his ear, "Just some more gay friends that Brian invited. Not to worry."

That seemed to calm him, but seriously, I still think the only reason I escaped a beating later that night is that my mother stayed overnight.

I DIDN'T KNOW IT, BUT the laptop Tony had given me for my 20th birthday had been rigged. He'd pre-installed a "child-safe" program that allowed him to monitor everything I did with it.

That was the first time I'd given any thought to him possibly spying on me, although I should have considered it way before then. I didn't say anything to him when I discovered it, and I didn't say anything when I found the tape recorder attached to the bottom of the bed stand, which I discovered only when it began clicking one day when I was lying on the bed reading. The tape had run out and hadn't shut off.

I left it there just as I'd found it.

Tony also hired a private investigator to follow me and another spy, who was a student at Hunter, to keep track of me when I was on campus.

I wasn't sure what I was going to do or how I'd approach the oh-so—volatile Tony, so I stayed quiet for the time being about all of it. I wasn't even as furious as I should have been. Perhaps I was in shock or I'd come to the realization that nothing was beyond this man. His jealousy would never stop.

A few days passed uneventfully. I was splitting my time between school and several modeling assignments, mostly fashion. Tony had been working late nights at the brokerage firm, but on this particular night, he'd asked his brother over to watch some sports event on television. (I will never forget this evening if I live to be a hundred!)

They were in the living room. I was doing my nails at the kitchen table. It was quiet until Tony suddenly burst into the room and shouted, "You bitch, you're sleeping with that fucking model from your party. You want to play me for a fool. I'll show you what I do to people who do that to me."

He lunged at me, grabbed me by my throat, and lifted me off the floor. Then he shook me. My feet dangled in midair. I felt like a ragdoll and thought I was going to choke to death.

My eyes felt like they were popping out of my head when his brother suddenly entered the kitchen, tapped Tony on the shoulder, and said, "Hey, stop it, bro. She's turning purple. Whatever she did, this isn't the way to deal with it."

Tony continued to shake me. The room went fuzzy. There was no more oxygen. Little bursts of light were filling my vision like miniature spots of lightning.

"Tony, let go! You're going to kill her!" I vaguely heard before I fell to the floor. Then I could feel the air coming back into me. *Thank God, I'm going to live!* Tony was standing over me. I was the vanquished foe, the big brother who always tortured him. Now he was getting even.

"You fucking bitch," he said again. "I'm going to kill that motherfucker. I saw your email that fucker sent with all that Portuguese bullshit code. I saw the picture of you and him at some party." He was maniacal again, out of control as he yelled and jabbed his index finger at me. He was on fire.

As the oxygen returned to my lungs, I could feel my hands and feet again. When he turned to his brother, I jumped up, grabbed my purse off the kitchen table, and made my escape out the door.

I ran down the hall as fast as I could, outdoors to the street. I glanced back. Tony wasn't there, but I kept running anyway, running until I was again out of breath.

After I was far enough away, I hailed a cab, not knowing where I would go. Piecing it all together, knowing he'd seen my emails, but also knowing there was nothing bad in them, I tried to figure out what he was enraged about—then it occurred to me that Rafael had sent me a message saying he'd had a great time at our party, that my "boyfriend" Tony was a great person, as were all my friends, and then he attached a picture someone took of us at the fashion show. He signed off, "Hope to work with you again."

His entire message was in Portuguese, which Tony didn't speak and the only visual was that one picture of us standing together next to one of the tables at the show.

After riding around in circles in the cab for about 15 minutes, I decided to call Brian. He always said to call him anytime, night or day, if I needed anything—and I really needed to be with someone sane; someone I knew was a friend.

I quickly dialed Brian's number. When he answered, I told him I was bored, that Tony was working late, and that I wanted to go see a movie with him. He said he had nothing to do and since he always liked talking with me about anything and everything under the sun, he accepted my invitation.

He chose *The Passion of the Christ*, not one I would've picked but we met in front of the theater about 30 minutes later nonetheless. The movie was *very* long, which gave me time to think.

After about half an hour, I told Brian I had to go to the restroom. I went out to the lobby and turned on my cellphone to, of course, find six or seven texts from Tony.

"Where are you, baby?"

"I'm sorry, baby."

"I translated that guy's email from Portuguese and see now that I was wrong."

"Come home, baby . . . please."

God, it all made me sick to my stomach. Loving man? Jealous maniac? Weakling who needed to bully others to feel strong himself? Which one was he? The obvious answer was—all of them. *I* was the most important thing to work on—*not* him—*me*! Why didn't I leave?

I didn't respond to any of his texts or messages, but turned off my phone and returned to the theater. When I sat down, Brian was crying—not loud enough for anyone to hear, but the tears were streaming down his face. He was so sensitive. I couldn't pay attention to the movie. It was too intense, and so was I. I wanted to forget Tony even existed. Even though Brian was obviously lost in the movie, my mind wandered away.

My agent had sent me a booking the day before. It was a Chris Brown music video that was going to be directed by Eric White, and the shoot would be in Los Angeles. My mind kept going back and forth between Tony and L.A. The part would be a lead role, playing a vampire that bites Chris on the throat, turning *him* into a vampire. I'd be flown out, of course, get my full day's fee plus per diem, and all other expenses. The shoot was two days away, which meant I'd have to fly out tomorrow.

Again, my mind jumped back to Tony. He would *never* let me do the shoot. My fledgling career was just starting to take off and I wanted to take advantage of every good job that came my way. Besides, why was I worried about what Tony felt?

I fidgeted in my seat. Brian was oblivious, tears still flowing. God he was sensitive!

Regardless of how Tony felt, I knew at this point, I still had to be smart. I had to get my things out of the apartment, so just taking off was out of the question. I asked Brian for his cellphone.

As he retrieved it from his shirt pocket, never losing eye contact with the movie, he didn't ask why I needed it when he knew that I had my own.

Again, I went out to the lobby this time to call my agent to confirm the shoot. Then, for fear it was hacked by Tony, I asked him not to call my cellphone and told him I would call him back in the morning to reconfirm and get all the additional information I needed.

Then I called Tony, preparing myself for what he would say.

"Oh, I'm so glad you called back. I was so worried, baby. When are you coming home?" he asked as if I'd just gone out to get groceries and nothing had ever happened, that he hadn't tried to strangle or kill me.

"Tony. You were *really* out of control this time. I did nothing wrong," I said, wanting to pull back those last four words as they left my mouth. Why was I explaining anything to him?

"Where are you?"

"I'm at the movies."

"Who with?"

None of your fucking business, I wanted to say. "With Brian. Who else?"

"I'm coming to get you."

"The movie will be over in an hour. I'll call you when I'm out front," I said. If I could have, I would have slammed down the receiver.

Finding my way back down the dark aisle of the theater, I sat down next to Brian again.

"What took you so long? Boy, the movie is really getting good. You're missing it," Brian said, full of excitement.

This time, I forgot to turn my phone completely off and the vibration alerted me to Tony's text. "I'm out front." I waited a moment, then told Brian that Tony was early, was out in front, and

I had to go talk with him. There were still about 20 minutes left of the movie so Brian said, "I'll talk with you tomorrow."

Once in the car, Tony was full of love again. "Did I hurt you, baby? Let me see," he said, pulling at the scarf I was wearing to cover up the bruises.

I took a deep breath. I didn't look at him, pretending instead to be interested in something outside. Then I said, "Tony, if you ever hurt me again, even so much as a pinch, so help me God, I will leave you."

The next morning after he left for work, I packed my things and took a taxi to the airport—no notes, no texts. When I got there, I bought a prepaid phone and left Tony a terse message on my old one that simply said, "Tony, I'm going to L.A. for a shoot."

MEN :(

I NSTEAD OF THE HEADING "Men," I wanted to use the old adage: "Men! Can't live with 'em and can't live without 'em." In Tony's case, however, I definitely wanted to live without him. I wanted him to be lying on the bottom of the East River with a 300-pound slab of concrete chained around his neck.

During one of the many, many nights I cried myself to sleep—not only for what Tony was doing and for who he was—but for me, not as the victim, but as the "fool" (to use his word).

People reading this book—and the thousands of other accounts of women being mistreated, abused, beaten, or killed—always ask, "Why didn't she just leave? She wasn't chained or behind bars."

I'll tell you the answer to that later, but for now just know it isn't as simple as it sounds. It not only involves one beast, it involves a willing party who is either so insecure or so scared (or both), that she is frozen emotionally—frozen into her own imagination of what life would be alone or what the beast might otherwise do.

One night, I had another of my crying spells and as I lay in bed feeling very angry with myself, my mind drifted back to a very sad story about my grandparents and great-grandparents in Brazil.

My father's mother, Ercy, had influenced me in many ways when I was growing up. The stories of her strength were legendary and when she shared them with me, she didn't think of herself as being strong—she just told them to me as lessons.

When I was very young, she told me a tragically true story that I'm sure will stay with me for the rest of my life. It was particularly poignant in light of my own situation.

Ercy married my grandfather when she was only 14. She had her first baby, Orlando, my uncle, when she was 16 and then my father came along when she was 17, which is why I have so many cousins.

My grandfather—another of those men who was filled with "machismo"—was in the army at the time. He was 22 when my father was born. According to Grandma Ercy, my grandfather was always jealous. But it wasn't just his machismo that made him that way; it was *her* beauty. With long silky black hair and skin like butterscotch cream, she was stunning. Her beauty became her curse, or so she says.

When my grandfather left for work every day, he would lock her inside the house with heavy chains on the door. She was literally a prisoner in her own humble home. In her time, things were different, especially in Brazil. Therefore, there was nothing she could do. Essentially and unofficially, since men controlled everything, including the culture, she was considered chattel.

One day they got into one of their many fights, only this one was worse than any other. He beat her badly. Ercy's parents, my great-grandparents, didn't know anything about the incident because she was frightened to death to tell anyone. Her father—another very macho, strict man—was also in the army. My grandmother was his princess. He would have done anything for her. When word got to him about what had happened, he arrived in a rage.

The fight that ensued was brutal. The two men started with their fists and then went to sticks and rocks and just about anything else they could get their hands on, including a gun. The worst thing possible happened when my great-grandfather pulled out his service revolver and shot my grandfather, who died later that day.

My great-grandfather went to jail for a few days as the *policia* investigated but because he was a famous general in the army, he was released with no further questions or actions. He wasn't truly free, however, because not long after, he drank himself to death over the guilt.

My grandmother had two little boys and now that their father was gone, she had to be strong for them. Needless to say, she matured quickly.

At 21, she met my future step-grandfather, Maia, who fell madly in love with the beautiful Ercy. Twelve years her senior, he was a successful lawyer in Rio. Several years after they were married, they had my Aunt Adrienne, who (as I mentioned earlier) is only five years older than I am.

Maia was a good father to the boys and a prince to my grandmother. For many years, no one told me he wasn't my real grandfather, but he was in so many ways.

When I was 17, Maia died of cancer—a very sad day for everyone who knew him. He was a mentor to many, especially me. He gave me so much good advice but probably the one thing that stuck with me the most was his thought about women: "A beautiful woman is a treasure, but a beautiful woman with brains is truly special." In those days, coming from a man of his culture, I didn't take that as some women would think today: *Oh, most beautiful women are stupid.* I knew what he meant and to me, that translated into getting an education.

Now, if I could just get out of this relationship with Tony!

On one particular night, Maia's thoughts were searing into my mind as I lay in bed wiping the tears away. "Suelyn," he would say, "you are very wise for your age. If you educate yourself and teach your brain great things, you will go far and be very happy."

He wanted me to go to law school, but I had no interest in law. My dream had always been medicine and now I was on a completely different track—psychology—but then perhaps not. Maybe I would be a different kind of doctor.

Goodbye to Tony

A s I was staring out the window of the enormous private plane, actually a converted 747, which in its commercial days carried more than 500 people to exotic destinations throughout the world, I began to reflect on my time with Tony.

When we met, I was 16 going on 17. I had been happy and full of life. I had a hunger to learn something new every day and to experience as much of life as it would throw at me, or vice versa. I'd even break everyday routines, if only to brush my teeth with my left hand one day and with the right on the next day, just to be different.

I also had a burning desire to be great at everything I did—not just good, but absolutely *the best*. I'm not sure where that came from; my parents were striving individuals, but not in this sense.

I try to excel in everything that interests me. I think that's what is at the heart of the overused word, passion. So many psychological "gurus" tell us to find our passion and then pursue it. With me, it was just the opposite. Passion would find me and then I would tear into each new endeavor as if my life depended upon it.

I love competitive sports, and while in Brazil immediately took to beach volleyball. I even had the chance to practice with the best AVP players in the world, received lessons from them, and even won some tournaments.

Now one of my favorite games, poker was another love. People tell me I have the best poker face and demeanor they've ever seen (usually after they've lost to me and I've won plenty of their money while playing).

Looking back, though, my desire to be the best started with my family and me. I always wanted to be the best daughter, granddaughter, sister, friend and even, one day, the best wife and mother. Having two younger sisters instilled a mothering instinct in me, rather than the bickering that is usually normal.

Therefore, it isn't a surprise to know that when I love, I love with all my heart, body, and soul, 100-percent. At first, when Tony came into my life, I was a little ambivalent, but it didn't take me long to warm up to his charm and "smarts." As our relationship grew, he seduced me, showed me a great deal of kindness, and professed his love to be "unconditional."

As time passed, however, and I shared my fears and dreams and he began to fully understand the things I loved the most, he also began a systematic and very patient campaign of control. I don't know if that had always been his plan or if it just happened, because he truly did love me as he became more and more jealous. Either way, his attempts to change everything about me, to mold me to his vision of a supplicating piece of arm candy, didn't work.

Eventually, as I put all the pieces together, I could see that he was trying to close one door after another, surrounding me with "him" and keeping the rest of the world at bay. His excuse for this was to "protect" me. His ammunition for this was to make me dependent upon him for everything. There were times I was suffocating, feeling I needed his permission to breathe.

Part of this insidious program, which many men deploy, is to give and then to take. Tony would shower me with gifts and attention. He would take me on trips. He would express his deep, intense love for me, and then he would turn mean and combative and try harder to isolate me, sometimes even hitting me . . . and then it would start all over again.

I'd told him from the very beginning that I cared about him, I liked him, and I loved the way he loved me; but, I was *not* in love with him, and certainly not enough to spend the rest of my life with him.

On those occasions, he would always respond with, "You love me. You just don't know it yet. It takes time for two people to develop into a full relationship."

Since I sensed his priorities early on, I repeated my mantra often—but he wasn't listening.

CHAPTER SIX

A New Man in My Life

I T WAS FINALLY TIME to leave Tony. Looking back with 20/20 vision, it was absolutely ridiculous the time that I spent with that man; but on a more positive note, I went through an enormous four-year learning curve. If I look at it that way, it was better than four years in college from the standpoint of going from 16 to 20, such an important age range, and all the life lessons learned. You can't get that kind of education living in a cocoon, and you can't learn those lessons (at least for me) without some psychic and physical wounds. Later, when you reflect, is when the lessons settle in. My decision was to go to California. What with the fashion world so much a part of that city, there were a lot of modeling opportunities in New York, but California offered Hollywood, movies, videos, music, and modeling options.

I needed a plan, though. I couldn't just go to my parents' house. Tony would locate me within an hour—and finding an apartment in New York was out of the question. With Tony's connections, he'd find me in a day, and I was more frightened than ever of what he would do when I took my freedom into my own hands.

I was doing a lot of modeling at the time—magazine covers, some videos and commercials—so I had a good portfolio with which to find work in California.

My thought was to get an apartment somewhere near L.A. and start over—just like that. I didn't know anyone there, but it didn't matter. The physical distance alone made me feel safer.

As I was planning my getaway, one of my agents called me about a gig in the Bahamas. A fashion designer owned an island there. He was letting people use it for the shoot, and a magazine was booking it for several days.

I'd heard about the island and its reputation for wild parties, so I was hesitant. My agent assured me that there would be a lot of people there: stylists, makeup, film crew, etc.

"Go down for two days. Have fun and make some money," she told me. "Everything is kosher."

I thought about it and finally called her back. "Go ahead and book it," I told her and the next week, I was flying down. My agent had told me the name of the designer that owned the island. At the time, I'd never heard of Peter Nygard, but outside of my small domain, he was enormous in the fashion world. Seems silly now to think that, in light of the successful empire he'd built at that time, I didn't know who he was.

His home base was in Toronto, Canada, but his products and influence were, and still are, worldwide.

I flew down with my agent and another model, Sarah, who is now a good friend. The photo shoot wasn't quite as organized or "professional" as my agent had painted it. It seemed more like a giant party, but it was only two days—so what could happen?

I learned that Mr. Nygard had requested me specifically, I guess from seeing some of my magazine work. I'd never been to a shoot like this; or in a place like this, for that matter. There were games on the beach organized by Mr. Nygard's staff, a lot of beer and alcoholic concoctions with umbrellas in them, and even more half-naked girls dancing in the sand. I was apprehensive. It seemed shady to me, a little "Bacchanalish."

I'd been working long enough now to know what goes on in a lot of photo shoots. There is almost the drug element, lots of liquor, and lots of lascivious men. I always approached my work professionally; perhaps I was naïve, but that was the way I wanted it.

After a day of the partying, I finally asked my agent, "When are we going to shoot?" I wasn't drinking (and I'm not pontificating right now; I say, everyone to his own devices) but when you're not drinking and everyone else is, and doing so quiet heavily, it isn't fun.

"Listen," I told my agent, "if there isn't going to really be a shoot, then I want to leave."

"No, Suelyn. This is the real deal. There's a dinner tonight. I want you to meet Peter. He's a great guy, and he's just trying to show everyone a good time. Be patient."

"Okay, I'll be patient, but I need to do the shoot tomorrow and then go home. I have a dinner thing in New York."

Sitting by the pool, sipping a Coke, Mr. Nygard suddenly appeared and sat next to me. He was trying to be very charming, and he was. He asked me all kinds of questions, telling me how beautiful he thought I was. I played along with it, giving him a coy smile and acting flattered while he was talking; but my thoughts were on a northbound plane.

I was also trying to let him know that I was all about business. I was, however, still on his turf and didn't want to be rude. The man had done nothing to me, personally. I also thought about all the girls here that would die to have his attention it for nothing else than the strings he could pull. However, that wasn't for me.

I had an argument later that day with my agent, during which I found out that the shoot was scheduled for four days, not two, and I became furious.

Finally, I went to Mr. Nygard and told him I had important family matters in New York. If we weren't going to get some serious business done, then I would find my own accommodations back.

When I told him I just didn't feel comfortable about the whole thing, he calmly replied, "That's okay. I understand. I'll have my staff book you on a flight out first thing tomorrow morning." I couldn't believe how gracious he was, how simple it was to just ask for what I needed and then get it.

The next morning I left for New York, glad to be done with the party scene. Within a couple of days, Mr. Nygard called me. After insisting that I call him Peter, we talked for a few minutes and he asked what my plans were for my career (knowing I was fairly new to it all), and I shared that I was moving to California for more opportunities. I didn't tell him about Tony.

I will admit that he was charming—he sounded kind, not aggressive—and seemed genuinely interested in me. He told me to stay in touch and to call him when I got to California, that he might be able to help me a little. He had a place in Marina Del Rey that was like his West Coast anchor.

I explained I was going to bring a friend and we were going to find an apartment. By that time, I'd already started on part of my plan, which was to wipe my name from everything. I got a new cellphone, a new number, and I didn't even give the post office my forwarding address. I canceled all the stores that I had accounts with whose bills would go to Hanover Square. Of course, my agent knew I was going to California, but even with her, I had no address yet.

At the time, Tony and my father were working on a huge project together, a supermarket in Queens. I had told my mother I was moving but not where. For the next couple of weeks, I would just call to let her know I was all right and that I would let her know where and when I was settled in. In some ways, it was faking my own death in terms of wiping out as much of my past information as possible, information that would lead Tony to me.

"Why are you looking for an apartment?" Peter asked.

"Well, obviously, because I need a place to live?"

"Excuse me, Ms. Suelyn, but I have homes everywhere, most of them empty. Why don't you stay in one of them? No strings attached. I have a beautiful little place in Marina Del Rey, right on the harbor. You could stay there. With the exception of furniture and a couple of housekeepers who live in the back, it's empty."

His "little" place was beginning to sound a little larger.

"I live in Canada or the Bahamas, so I don't use it much. Stay for a couple of weeks, at least until you find your own place," Peter said.

It didn't sound like a bad idea, especially the "no strings attached" part. I wouldn't have to make any hasty choices on my own place. "Listen," Peter continued, "if you're going to do some more work on my line, we'll need to talk anyway, probably often. You are interested in working for my line, aren't you?"

He'd caught me off-guard. Although his clothing was stunning, absolutely top-notch and known all over the world, I hadn't given any thought to working with him.

"Leave whenever you want," he added, "but take advantage of the beach and the weather and get a little more acclimated, then go look for your apartment."

I had to admit, he was convincing. I really had nothing to lose and he could be an incredible boost to my career with his own line and all his connections.

The kicker was when he offered to fly me (and all of my things) out on his private plane.

"Listen, Suelyn. I have a private plane. You could put all your things on that and make the move in one fell swoop."

While the ease of it all excited me, I was still worried about Tony. Because of my mood change, he'd sensed something was up with me. I figured I would wait until I knew he was at work all day so I told Peter, "Yes, thank you. I will take you up on both offers. No strings attached," I added.

While packing, I was very nervous. I knew I couldn't take everything. Peter was even going to send a limo to Hanover Square to pick it all up. I was well aware that I'd have to travel light, and I didn't want to take a lot of memories along with me anyway. I left all the jewelry, all the things I'd brought into the apartment. Basically, I stuffed all of my good clothes, toiletries, and makeup into four large suitcases.

Peter's plane—a 727, the same used to fly 300 people across the country—was enormous. When we landed in California, and I got my bags; another limo driver met me and whisked me off to Marina Del Rey. The house was stunning, a mansion. I was introduced to the staff of maids, cooks, housekeepers, and a man who just took care of all of Peter's cars.

I was speechless. The home was right on the beach and the day was spectacular. Being able to walk right out the front door onto the beach immediately reminded me of Brazil. I loved beach volleyball and swimming—all competitive sports, really—so I was in heaven. What a difference from New York!

Peter wasn't there, of course, but I was shown to a spectacular room, one that was all my own to do with as I pleased. I'd let my agent know what my plans were so by the time I got settled in, I had several jobs lined up. She was booking magazines, music videos with the top groups at the time, and commercials.

By now, I was becoming diversified into different markets. The Latin, Urban, American, and Brazilian markets had different demographics with different likes, wants, and needs when it came to music, television, clothing, food—you name it.

The key was to appeal to each market individually and as intimately as possible, as though that market's consumer was my only client base.

Additionally, because of that diversity, I now had different agents and promoters for each market, people who knew those markets intimately. But the big difference between me and others is that I controlled everything. I didn't have an entourage of hangers-on that didn't necessarily have my best interests at heart. Everyone around me made good money, and we all worked hard and honestly together.

I have to admit, however, that as I got busier and busier, scheduling became a nightmare. Oftentimes, with so many opportunities in different markets all at the same time, it took a team to take advantage of everything that was top-notch, professional, and aboveboard.

I also had to admit, there were many people who wanted to "manage" me but most turned out to be more interested in dating. I knew I could manage myself just fine, so that's what I continue to do to this day.

We've all heard the stories: for example, the professional boxer who has more talent than he knows what to do with and a morass of managers hanging on to him, looking for every dollar that drops out of his pocket, and some that have to be wrenched from his checkbook. There are financial managers, talent managers, booking agents, and even managers that want to manage the other managers. It's endless, and they will eat you up if you let them.

I've had to choose very carefully. I like to control my assignments, where my pictures will be seen, how they will be seen and, of course, my own checkbook.

I take it all seriously. Because of that, and because it is a business like any other, some people see me as being rude, abrupt, short-tempered, or even a bitch, but that's just a shell I use to protect the real me. If I am not engaged in business, then I am very open and engaging. In fact, I'm told by people who don't threaten me, that I'm very shy. It's just two different mindsets.

In the business mode, I stay three steps ahead of everyone. They may think I don't know where they're going with an issue or what they mean, but I've already thought the pros and cons out, and researched it all.

I'm fascinated with people that want to grow, that want to make something out of nothing. Another thing that I have learned along the way is to always surround myself, not only with honest people, but with people smarter than me, especially in areas that I've experienced. I have never claimed to know it all. Everyone, all the way to the President of the United States, needs a smart team.

By the time I'd been in Marina Del Rey for about three weeks, I'd already shot eight magazine covers. My portfolio was bulging and I became an avid collector of all of them—not out of ego, but because anything tangible like a magazine, DVD, movie, or even a commercial—were proof to me that I existed. That sounds odd, I know, but all of those accounts affirmed my belief in *me*.

The more jobs that came in nearly every week, the more selective I was able to be, until I got to the point where I felt safe financially and could turn down anything I didn't like, was suspicious of, or didn't think would help my career.

Back to Peter's Place

I was so grateful to Peter for letting me stay in his home. Just as he'd said when we first talked about my move to California, he was rarely there. We did talk once in a while over the phone, but mostly I was either working or just enjoying some time off at the beach. He became a sort of "phone mentor," always telling me to shoot for the stars and to be careful to take myself to the next level, but in the right way. "Save your money," he always admonished me. "That nest egg will be a part of your confidence. You'll always know you can support yourself and you've got back up. Having a lot of money in the bank means you can turn down things you don't need."

Three weeks went by when Peter called and said he was doing a fashion tour in the U.S. He was going to start in New York. He was also building a new center, a design facility and offices on 42nd Street—a fashion tower, he called it.

During one of our calls, he told me he wanted me to be the main model on the tour. He asked me to check my schedule and said I would be getting a very nice daily rate and a bonus, all of which he'd deposit by wire transfer in advance in my bank account. The tour would last almost two weeks, so I had to block out a lot of potential work, but it would be more than worth it.

The following week I went to New York. Peter had arranged rooms at the W for all the models. At night, we all got together and had dinner somewhere trendy and very nice. He spared no expense, either then or in the entire time I've known him.

The fashion tour started in New York, went to Washington and Baltimore—all the big cities on the upper eastern seaboard. In the mornings, we'd all get up early, have a meeting to structure the day, figure out the clothes we'd wear, and then board a big tour bus. It was like a political or rock tour. There was a different city every day.

People would greet the bus, because to those women 30 and older—women who adored his clothes—Peter was a celebrity.

I knew Peter also wanted someone to represent his line that could talk during meetings and with the buyers and consumers. I, in turn, was fascinated with his business acumen, how he wanted to go completely high-tech in his design center by putting in a lounge where the women could drink coffee, tea, or wine while they were shopping; by using large flat-screen displays for pictures of the clothes; or running past videos, among many other innovations.

I was learning so much from this man. Forty years my senior, he was my mentor. We talked about books endlessly, new designs, philosophy—you name it. He had taken me under his wing. Our friendship grew on a daily basis.

One of my favorite pastimes was playing poker with him, especially Texas Hold-Um, at which I was a natural. He could stay up all night and lose money to me. I don't know how he did it. At the time, he was well into his 60s and he rarely slept, or at least it seemed that way to me.

When the tour ended, we stayed in New York a few days. From all of our conversations on airplanes, playing poker, dinner, or on breaks from work, we talked incessantly. He wanted to know everything about me, my family, my background. When I told him my father was in construction, he got this crazy idea to hire him to work on his new building in Times Square.

I didn't think that was such a good idea but didn't tell him so. My father was into residential construction or small retail buildings, nothing even close to what Peter was doing. Besides, I could only imagine what would happen if he worked with my father, who was also working with Tony—definitely the makings of a total disaster. And, I didn't want to tell Peter that my father was in the country illegally. Peter was a real "on the books" kind of guy. Everything was always straight and legal. He also did not drink or smoke.

I tried to change the subject, but when we got back to California, Peter brought it up again. For some reason, he wanted to put my father to work, and he wasn't going to let it go. So, I called my father and told him briefly what was happening, but I also told him that he could not say a word to Tony about it.

When the two did meet for about an hour, Peter hired my father to work on his building. I'm not sure what he did, or even if Peter was just giving him work to make me happy and help my family but whatever his motives, my father went to work for him in New York.

It was then that I told my parents I was living in California, was doing very well, and that I didn't want them to be involved with Tony in any way, shape, or form. In fact, I wanted them to move to California to be close to me.

The only caveat seemed to be that my father wanted to finish a supermarket project with Tony. It was his duty, he said, his commitment, for which I respected him. My father always lived up to his promises. Even so, I still felt hesitant about him continuing to work with Tony, who wasn't a stand-up kind of guy. He'd been involved with his brother's drug scam; they'd even rented a house in New Jersey to work out of and stash the drugs. He had a shady past with his credit; he hired spies; and he was also, of course, very volatile. I didn't trust him as far as I could throw his Mercedes.

For the next six months, my father continued working with Tony to finish the project. I was filled with stress over what could happen at almost any given moment. I wanted my father's deal with Peter to work and for my family to move out close to me so I could help take care of my mother and sisters.

During that time, Tony began to look for me in earnest. He didn't have my number and my family told him nothing, but he managed to find one of my email addresses. I began to get notes from him about how much he still loved me, how he'd lost weight, all the deals he was making—just pages and pages of things. I never answered a single one, but since they didn't bounce back to him undeliverable, he knew they were reaching me.

The interesting thing, or rather the sad, sad thing, is that I really still hadn't grown as far as I thought. I'd been working a great deal, learning a lot about the world of business, traveling, and getting to know very sophisticated people and yet, here I was reading this idiot's email diatribes. There was no love whatsoever. There was really nothing more than disdain. I didn't even hate him, because I felt he was so stupid, so narcissistic, so cruel and yet, I was still drawn to reading his letters.

Curiosity always kills the cat.

It was what is was. I couldn't figure out myself or my motives. Perhaps it was just curiosity. Then Tony's notes grew even more threatening, alternating between loving and/or wanting to kill me. Sick. Sick. *Sick!*

Eventually, I grew bored with it all. It was kind of like the tabloid magazines that grab your attention in the supermarket checkout lines—you know it's all lies, but you look at them anyway, and plenty of people actually buy them!

I continued to work a great deal and talked with my family two or three times a week by phone, just waiting for the day that he would be finished with Tony's job so they could come out to California.

Then, one night I got a horrible phone call from my mother. She was crying uncontrollably.

"Mom, what is it? Why are you crying?"

She could barely speak.

"Sue, your father never came home last night. He was going to stop and pick up dinner, but he never came home," she sobbed.

It was January, so in New York it was snowing and extremely cold. It was also already midnight there.

"Okay, Mom. Try to calm down. Let's call the hospitals."

"Sue, I've already called his cellphone. It's going into voicemail. I've called everyone from his job. I even called Tony; he knew nothing."

"Okay, Mom. I'm going to call the hospitals. Say a prayer. Everything will be all right. I'll call you back soon."

I looked up every hospital in Queens and began calling. None of them had a record of admitting a Sergio Mederios. My next thought, though I didn't want to try it, was to call the police. When I connected with the various precincts, I tried my father's real name and then asked them if any other men had been picked up on immigration charges. The answer was no every time.

I called my mother back. I tried to calm her down and told her to try to get some sleep, that I had a friend who would look into it first thing in the morning. Then at 4:00 a.m. Pacific Time, my mother called again. My father had called her; he'd been arrested by immigration, which is why the police had no record. Someone had called them and given them an anonymous tip. I knew immediately it had been Tony. Who else would know so much about my father? Who would care? He was a quiet man who went about his work methodically every day and then went home to his family. That was it.

PETER'S PERKS CONTINUED. He'd given me a Ferrari to drive, red of course, and it was completely mine to use as I wished, minus the title. He also gave me free reign to drive the BMW X-5 SUV, the Hummer, and a Delorean—the one with the gull-winged doors, all shiny polished aluminum and fast that they used in the *Back To The Future* movie—which was a collector's item.

I'd been living in his house in Marina Del Rey for four months at that point and my career was really taking off. That Saturday night, I'd been invited to the Espy Awards (ESPN). The previous year, I'd "worked" the event as one of those models who came out from the back in a long elegant dress to hand out the awards. By that time, I'd also shot a commercial for the Super Bowl and the World Cup. This time, however, I'd be walking in the front door as a celebrity guest. Since I wasn't dating, I asked a friend, a pretty blonde, to come with me. Together we made a good statement. I had on a cream-colored Herve Ledger dress and gold, five-inch Versace heels. Diamond studs sparkled on my ears with a bling ring on my right hand to round out my jewelry. I felt like a million bucks with my long silky black hair that bounced off my shoulders like the tail of an expensive show horse.

When I was ready to go, I went into the garage and surveyed the cars neatly arranged on the shiny, surgically-clean concrete floor. *Eenie, meenie, minie, moe*, I thought, then decided to take the Delorean.

In short, for my career, I wanted to be seen. A lot of people in Hollywood wanted to attend, but I had front row seats and didn't have to go as someone's candy.

Just like at the Academy Awards, there was a red carpet walk and, of course, I strutted my stuff slowly all the way down to the entry doors. Lights were flashing and reporters asked for interviews. Even while effecting a slight air about myself—all the while keeping a nice smile, with my eyes open wide—I was glad to oblige.

The awards ended around 10:00 p.m., which is when I began to see friends, athletes, models, and others I'd met through the last couple of years. We all decided to go out for drinks together. We met at a club down the street, where I had parked the Delorean with the valet, and went inside. My girlfriend was supposedly not far behind, although I had my doubts since she'd been talking to an athlete when we left the theater.

Once inside, everyone was doing shots, laughing and talking, and having a good time. After two rounds, I decided to leave. I'm not much of a drinker and I didn't want to drive under the influence. However, being the one who never wants to arrive first or leave last, I stayed longer, which was a big mistake. After several other people left, I knew it was time to segue out gracefully. We'd been there for three hours, and even though I'd had four shots, I felt I was okay.

Wrong.

As the valet brought the car around and both doors swung open, a casual friend, Claudia, standing nearby saw all the attention I was getting from the press and approached me as if we were best friends.

"Oh hi, Suelyn. It's been a while. You're looking great . . .," (yada, yada, yada), she gushed and then asked for a lift.

"Hi, Claudia. I'm just going to a hotel down the street. I can't drive all the way to the Marina tonight. I've had a few too many," I answered, thinking the ride would be too short for her, But she jumped in anyway, all the while using her cellphone to take pictures of all the celebrities, the car, and me.

The hotel was less than three blocks away. I should have just left the car at the club and picked it up in the morning but *noooooo*, I had to drive.

As I pulled out onto Hollywood Boulevard and made a right turn, I was immediately caught in the lights of a police cruiser, siren squawking, and an officer's voice over the cruiser's loudspeaker. "Pull over to the curb," which I did, reaching into the glove box for the registration.

I sat calmly waiting for the officer to come to the window. As he approached, he menacingly said, "Get out of the car!" I dutifully did so and closed the door while Claudia giggled and took pictures.

"Okay. Stand still," the officer said. "Have you been drinking?" I told him that I'd had two drinks about two hours ago—which was not the right thing to say.

"Okay, I'm going to do a field sobriety test on you. I need you to walk with one foot in front of the other, a straight line from here over to that car," he instructed as he pointed to a car parked at the curb several feet in front of the Delorean.

I knew I was in trouble. Not only had I had four drinks, but I was wearing five-inch heels, which weren't exactly stable.

"Officer, I have on very high heels. It's difficult to walk in them."

"Okay. Take them off."

Not what I wanted to hear. To make matters much worse, instead of just walking barefooted, I had to act like a fool and do a "runway" style sashay, throwing my hips back and forth, laughing and trying to be cute. (Ah, the naivete of youth!)

The officer was not impressed. He quickly put handcuffs on me and crammed me into the backseat of the cruiser. Looking back at the Delorean, I saw that Claudia had gotten into another car with a friend. She never said a word or offered to drive the Delorean home.

What I didn't realize at the time was that I was being taped.

Arriving at the station, I took off all my jewelry, which a female officer put in a plastic bag in my purse, and then wrote my name on it with a Magic Marker.

"Officer," is there any insurance I can buy to cover these if someone steals them?" I asked. At the time, probably not the best question to ask, but in the less-than-sharp-condition I was in, it seemed plausible to me at the time. The officer, of course, looked at me and merely rolled her eyes. *Oh boy! Another Lohan.*

I went through the booking procedure where they fingerprint you and then take your picture, just like in the movies. In real life, however, it isn't pleasant. From there, I was taken down a long, cement hallway, past several cells, each with several women in them, separated from me by a heavy steel door and a large thick window. As you might guess, they all looked quite depressed. The walls, floor, and ceiling were all the same dull gray.

Before I was marched down the hall, I was told not to look around but to do what the officer instructed. There were three colored lines—yellow, green, and black—about four inches wide on the floor At the end of the hall, they all split off into different directions.

"Stay on the yellow line," the officer barked, and I did. I was beginning to get it as the alcohol was wearing off. As I said earlier, I rarely drank anything and if I did, it was some concoction with an umbrella that I nursed for hours. I should have known better. Instead, I was too caught up in what I thought was my own celebrity, and the fun and action of the evening. (I was as star struck as anyone at the Epsys, but I never would have let anyone know that.)

As I continued down the yellow line, I began to see why being incarcerated can really sober you up, not just in that moment or night, but for a long time after (if you're smart).

At the end of the hall, the yellow line turned to the left.

"First cell on your right. Stand there facing the door. Do not touch it. Keep your hands at your sides," the officer ordered.

She removed a large key from her pocket, told me to stand back, and then slipped the key into the lock. When she pulled it back, the door squeaked as if it hadn't been opened in a hundred years, but the three women I saw inside attested otherwise.

"Step inside."

I took two steps and was inside with the women; one looked like a hard-core hooker, which would not have been out of the ordinary given that this was Hollywood. Another looked like she was a kick-boxer, and the third was just sobbing into her hands. All of them sat on a block of concrete that ran the length of the rear wall. In the corner was a steel toilet with a steel sink—all one piece. There was no toilet paper.

I will *hold it.*

As I diverted my eyes, I sat as far away from the other three as I could manage without being too obvious. I took a deep breath. *What happens now?*

My first thought was to keep to myself. My second thought was, *How can I call Peter to get me out? Will they even let me out? For all*

I know, I'll have to sit here until I'm taken to court, and Lord knows when that'll be! I figured my best bet was to keep my mouth closed and wait, so I didn't ask the others.

After about five minutes, one of the women approached me and asked, "What's wrong, pretty lady?" as she flicked my hair with her index finger. Then she started laughing in a maniacal sort of way. When she sat back down, another of the women approached and sniffed my neck like a dog about to mark its territory.

"What is it?" she asked.

"What is what?" I replied.

"The perfume, cutie."

"Uh, it's Angel," I responded. With that, she started to laugh, which started the other two laughing as this woman finished with, "Yeah, but ain't no angels getting out of here." Then, she ran her filthy hands and fingernails (that obviously hadn't seen a cleaning in months) through my hair.

"Don't touch me!" I said, but not with *too* much authority. "Just leave me alone," I said, pushing my hair back over my shoulders.

Remembering all the movies I'd seen, it was time to figure out what I was going to do. There was a small slot in the door. I went to it, yelling out to no one in particular, "When do I get to make my call?"

I waited. No answer.

Two of the women come up behind me and started picking at my blouse, and laughing and poking at me. I thought I was going to either explode or faint when an officer suddenly appeared. Seeing what was going on, she unlocked the door and told the two women to step back. She then escorted me out of that cell and put me in another one by myself.

A deep sadness came over me. Again, I could see clearly why people who do stupid things are incarcerated: one, for punishment; two, to save them from themselves and others; and, three, to give them time to think about what they've done. Unfortunately, sometimes that takes a lifetime; other times, just one night. Either way, I did some very serious thinking. I began to think about what it would be like to spend months or years in such a place, deprived of my freedom or of seeing my parents and sisters again. I also began to relive all the bad things I'd done in my life going back as far as I could remember, to when I started the fire in my uncle's garage when I was just 4—everything.

It was a long, awful night of reflection. Finally, an officer came to the door of the cell (I don't know what time it was) and said I could make my call. She took me to a small room where there was a phone on the wall and told me I had three minutes.

It was then that I realized I didn't have my cellphone with all my contacts. The only two numbers I'd memorized were my grandmother's in Brazil (out of the question); Tony's (even *more* out of the question); and three, Peter's (also out of the question). That's when I started to cry for the first time since being arrested. What a fool I'd been.

"You now have only one more minute left," the officer said as I sat inert on the chair.

"Could I have a phonebook?" I asked her. "I don't have my cellphone and I need a number."

"No. And, again, you only have one more minute left."

I was at a dead end, without being able to make my call. The officer took me back to my cell. By this time, I knew it had to be very late and, surrounded by nothing but concrete, it was also getting very cold, especially since I only had on a tube top and my lightweight Herve dress. Unlike the first one, there was a bed in this cell, along with a nasty dark green, wool blanket that looked and smelled like 10 years of pee had soaked up through the fibers.

After another fit of crying, I somehow managed to fall asleep. It seemed only a few minutes had passed when I heard banging on the cell door. It was morning and an officer was calling my name. "Suelyn Medeiros, you have a visitor."

Who can it possibly be? Maybe Claudia told someone I had been arrested. Maybe it's her.

I jumped up and went to the door to see a man I didn't recognize.

"Hello, Ms. Medeiros. I'm Jacob. I'm a bail bondsman. *TMZ* told me you were arrested last night. I'm here to bail you out. Others are working on your papers right now. It will only be another hour or so," and with that, he left.

In the ensuing hour, I was escorted out to a reception area where they returned my bag of goodies and shoes. I immediately took out my phone to call Morten, the housekeeper, to come and get me. As we drove back to Marina Del Rey, I looked at my phone. I had 50 missed calls, 22 voicemails, and I don't know how many texts.

The first call I returned was to my friend, Britt, who said, "Oh my God, Suelyn. What happened to you? It's all over the Internet how you got drunk and got a DUI."

Oh God, I thought, holding my hand to my forehead.

"The video of your arrest is online. It wasn't as bad as Mel's, though," she finished before hanging up.

Later, as I cringed and watched it all on TV, the *TMZ* film showed the entire thing; me sashaying around like a runway model, acting like an idiot, and laughing. It was horrible. The title was: "Brazilian Model Suelyn Hottest DUI Arrest." I was more than embarrassed. I was mortified. The first thing I thought of was my sisters—how I wanted to set good examples for them and wanted to be the best sister, daughter, and even mother one day. Then it occurred to me: This is forever. This is on the Internet. Someday, my children will see me like this.

Douglas Again

MY RELATIONSHIP WITH DOUGLAS was an on-and-off-thing again. I never really opened my heart to him because I was afraid it wasn't safe to do so. He was *very* macho and *very* Brazilian, and he hated that I'd moved in with Peter. To him, nothing was ever "free" or that I didn't have to do anything in return.

"Why would he do all that for you and get nothing in return?" was Douglas's mantra. Although admittedly, I liked him very much, his comments and insinuations hurt me and played a strong role in why I didn't open my heart to him.

Typically, after one of such comments, we would fight, he would leave, and we wouldn't talk for a while. Besides, he was very busy with his career as was I with mine. In time, we would see each other again and even date. At one point, he even took me to Brazil to meet his mother and brother and when we returned, I introduced him to my mother and sisters in New York.

Douglas had many issues; chief among them were drugs. He never used around me, but I knew—and it bothered me and was a huge turnoff, pushing me away from him even more. In fact, that summer, I used the big "F" word by telling him that I just wanted to be "friends." He didn't take it well, but he had no choice.

Soon afterward, he and I were doing a TV show for a Brazilian channel. We shot a few episodes in Brazil, Europe, and Los Angeles; and we were actually becoming good friends. He still wanted to be romantically involved, but he was being a good sport.

Later, closer to the holidays, he booked a movie deal in Portugal and invited me to go with him, but I was busy, involved in other projects, and Christmas was only a week away.

I planned to go to New York to spend the holidays with my mother and sisters, and then we were planning to drive down to Virginia where my father was being transferred to a new facility.

Because my mother's birthday is on the 23rd of December, it always seems to be overshadowed by Christmas so, this time, I wanted to do something special for her. We had a big party and were all having fun when my cellphone rang. It was an unidentified caller, which I never answer. Then it rang again. This time it was an unavailable caller, so I answered, not wanting it to keep ringing. Turns out, it was someone on the cast of the movie Douglas was shooting.

"Are you Suelyn?" the voice asked.

"Yes, what is it? I'm busy."

"I'm with the cast of a movie that we are filming with a friend of yours, Douglas?" he questioned to make sure he had the right Suelyn.

"Yes, what is it?"

"Miss, I'm sorry to tell you that Douglas is dead."

Oh my God! A shockwave ran through my entire body. I was stunned, couldn't catch my breath.

"Wh-what? H-how?" I stammered

"I'm sorry. This is difficult for both of us, but they found him floating in the river. There are signs of a possible strangling. We need to get in touch of his family, and I saw your number in his phone."

My world stopped. I began to cry. He was so young and he was my friend.

When I returned to Los Angeles the next day to help his brother gather Douglas's things, that's when it hit me—the guilt, the what ifs. *What if I'd gone to Portugal? Would he still be alive? What if I'd been a better friend?* These thoughts were gut-wrenching for me.

Helping his brother pack his things was one of the most difficult days of my life. I couldn't believe he was gone—just like that! I started remembering our last conversation and how we left off—how sweet he was and how cold I was.

I knew I was being selfish, but as the days dragged forward, all I could think of was how I could be a better person, more forgiving, forget the little things, look to the more important things in life, and see the good in everyone. It was a long, *long* two weeks until I got myself back to being somewhat "normal." When I did, I tried to focus on how fleeting life is; how it can be snuffed out in the blink of an eye; and how we sometimes don't appreciate those around us until they're gone.

I vowed I wouldn't take my friends lightly ever again. I would be more forgiving. I would laugh with them every chance I got and see nothing but the good in them. I would be patient.

A RIO NEW YEAR

WHILE RIO IS PERHAPS better known for its Carnival, the New Year celebration is easily as much fun, if not more. In 2006, Peter wanted to plan something very special for our New Year, so he asked me what I'd like to do. "The sky's the limit," he said.

There was no hesitation on my part. "RIO!" I said enthusiastically.

Peter reached into the breast pocket of his jacket, withdrew his wallet, and handed me his black American Express card. "Here. Book it, Dano," he said smiling, knowing how happy it made me. "Bring your friends, too," he added.

It was almost as much fun setting up all the arrangements as I knew it was going to be to actually go. With flights, hotel, ground transportation, and ten people or more to plan for, I felt like an air traffic controller in the tower at JFK airport. When the dust settled, the invitation list included five of my girlfriends, four of Peter's friends, two photographers, and an assistant—12 in all.

I chose the Copacabana Palace, the most expensive, luxurious, and hippest resort in Rio de Janeiro. The suites went for $40,000 for the New Year's week package, and the tickets to the Grand Ball were $1,500 each. (There were two to a room, so you can do the math.)

At nearly the last minute, I also arranged for Dayane to join us on New Year's Eve night. Knowing that this was going to be *the* ultimate experience for all of us, I was caught up in the whirlwind of expectation. From rising in the morning until the last thing I did before I went to bed at night, I was organizing, planning, and making adjustments because there were also the daily activities to plan for everyone—everything from sight-seeing the Cristo and the Sugar Loaf Mountains, to parasailing, paint-balling in the Brazilian forest, as well as other entertaining events. Since money was obviously not an issue, I had the deluxe smorgasbord of things from which to choose.

Peter was impressed with my skills. Far more complicated than even a large wedding, I organized it all. Where he needed a staff of people to plan his small events, there was just me to make all the arrangements for the biggest thrill of the year.

Everything was moving smoothly, perhaps too smoothly. You know when you get that feeling that you try to push out of your mind, when it's all going so well, you just know something's going to happen? Well, I was right because my grandmother in Brazel had a stroke. Needless to say, my mother was beside herself and I was stunned, so Peter invited my mother to come with us on his private jet so she could see her mother.

The two-story plane was a 727, that could normally seat 300 people, but with the customized interior, bedrooms, bar, kitchens, etc., it could easily accommodate 100 in supreme comfort. It was like being inside a large condo. As we stood on the tarmac and I saw it for the first time, I remember thinking, *How does this thing get off the ground?* It was my first time in a private plane going to Brazil.

The flight took about 8 hours but the time passed quickly as if I were with my friends in my own living room. The flight was so smooth and quiet, if you were blindfolded, you wouldn't know you were in a plane flying at 35,000 feet.

After checking in at the Copacabana, I supervised each guest personally, taking them to their rooms and getting them settled. Then, I took a break and went to the hospital to visit my grandmother. The right side of her body had been paralyzed and her speech and hearing had been affected, but the doctors said she was lucky to be alive and that, with therapy, she would get better.

My mother stayed with her the rest of that day. Once I knew she was stable and comfortable, I returned to the hotel.

That night, I handed out the week's schedule to everyone. Our first stop that evening was dinner at a hot nightclub. Throughout the week, the two photographers followed us. They must have shot a mile of video and thousands of stills of everyone having the time of their lives—enough to fill a hundred scrapbooks.

New Year's Eve day, the girls had monopolized a nearby salon, getting their nails, makeup, and hair ready for the big evening. In Brazil, it's a tradition to wear white on this holiday because we believe it's a way of starting the year fresh and pure, a new beginning. No matter where I am, I still follow this tradition.

My dress was as white as newly fallen snow, accented with white shoes to match and diamond jewelry.

After dinner, there was a phenomenal 30-minute fireworks' display punctuated by the countdown to midnight. When the clock struck 12, Peter turned to me and gave me a light kiss on the lips. I immediately froze but so that I wouldn't embarrass him, I smiled, tittered like a little girl, and went off to join my friends who were dancing.

Dayane was starry-eyed all night. She'd never experienced anything like our extravaganza. Her family was very poor so it bordered on the overwhelming.

Peter noticed how close I was with her. He'd never seen me that way with anyone and so I was surprised when he suggested, "Suelyn, I can see how much you care for your cousin and I remember what you told me about her circumstances. What would you think about taking her to live in the U.S.?"

I was so speechless, my mouth fell open. When I finally recovered, I told him I'd tried to get her a visa earlier but it was declined.

"Not to worry. I will make some calls and we will take her with us if that's what you'd like to do."

"Peter, it would fulfill a childhood dream."

Dayane had always dreamed of going to America and within 24 hours, Peter made it happen. He got her a visa as a flight attendant on his plane so she was able to return with us. I was so excited because I now had my buddy—my partner in crime—with whom to play.

Dear Diary,

@ ^^ # ^^ *&%* (**@~~~@ ##^^^##@9 *)__++
##@^^^%%%6 **^^—) 00 {{{# @@!!.

That is how my diary entry began when I was 21. At the time, I would have been humiliated if anyone had been able to read it. Now, it's different because this is my story—warts and all—so now I can tell it in English. It's interesting how our "wisdom" comes upon us. Sometimes people have to get old to gain it. Sometimes, if you're lucky, you get glimpses or insights along the way. In my case, I learned a lot of valuable lessons early on, at a younger age than most, but maybe that's just because I was living in an older world (not to be confused with a more enlightened world).

Diary entry: March 2003

Responsibilities are thrust upon us, but we also ask for them. Today, I feel weighed down by my obligations. At times, being 21 seems so grown up and yet, on an emotional level, I know differently.

Today, it feels difficult for me to breathe.

I am in my room at Peter's enormous house. That in itself is almost overwhelming when these wide-open spaces are not mine but are, instead, a constant reminder that I owe him—all the time.

Friends say, "What a wonderful life. Everything is free, and you don't have to do anything."

With even a little of that precocious wisdom, I know better. I fear and know that the day of reckoning (aka: payback) is coming, sooner than later. Nothing is free, but you can get a lot of it if you're not careful what you ask for; and, then, when you least expect it, if/ when you're not prepared, it'll be time to pay the piper.

What will he ask of me? What will I have to do? I feel like I'm being saved for some enormous task or emotional investment that I won't be able to handle.

I am standing on the tracks near the third rail. Now that my father is in prison again, and my mother and sisters only have me, the weight of that responsibility is monumental. Of course, I never share this with anyone. I must be as brave as I have always been, a problem solver, the "get it done" girl. I have to provide for them. My mother has never worked, and she is so weak without my father there to handle everything. She's spent her adult life being protected. And my sisters are too young.

I wonder what a psychiatrist would say about my guilt. I should know, but I don't, even though I am studying psychology. Instead, I write in my journal, which, in many ways, is like talking to a shrink—the doctor only listens, as does this blank page. Then it is up to me to "hear" my own solutions from what I am saying or writing.

Not easy.

If I leave Peter's now, providing for them and myself will be too much. I can't afford it. When my phone rings and I see it's a call from my mother, I get butterflies in my stomach and not the good ones like a first kiss. I immediately feel sick, almost nauseous.

What will she need? Can I do it, handle it, get it for her? Is it going to be an emergency? Is she hurt? Are the girls okay? On and on. She calls me for everything big and small. I always answer. It's never anything good. *When do I get the good news? When will she ask me how I am, what I am doing, or how my career is going?*

In psychology studies, "they say" that guilt and anger are closely aligned. My guilt now turns to anger. I can feel it as I'm writing.

Why can't she just once deal with something, solve some problems, starting with a minor one? I love her. I love my family with every fiber of my being down to the cellular and up to the highest spiritual levels—*but* . . . and that's always the word that negates everything prior to it—*but*, I feel like they are sucking me dry. I feel like they are all drowning and they've managed to find a small piece of wood (me) floating in their vast ocean of need, and all three of them are clinging to it for dear life. But that piece of wood can only support so much weight. No matter how buoyant it is, there *is* a limit.

Who is there for me? And worse, *what if something happens to me so that I can't take care of them?* (Guilt followed by anger followed by guilt—oftentimes, it's a seemingly endless loop. *Who will have my back?* I'm 21 and while my friends are worrying about what dress to wear to the party, I am worried about money. How much money will I have on the first of the month to put toward my mother and sisters' rent. What about the utilities, the phone, food? We are, of course, grateful for the help my mother gets from the government but, unfortunately, it's a mere raindrop in the ocean.

Now my mother is faced with Lupus—a terrible thing, an insidious, long-term thing—and there are drugs to pay for and treatments. My sisters need her to be as strong as possible. I need her, too, but not for strength.

My career is so uncertain. I'm booking a lot of work now; but if that dries up, what then? I came to live at Peter's temporarily. It was a two-edge sword—survival and growth in a tenuous partnership. Survival, which is getting away from crazy Tony. Growth—learning, career, independence—which is funny because I have no independence. I am free of Tony and know I'll never be trapped again, if that's the consolation prize, but now I'm trapped as a result of my own ingenuity. Trapped by a man's generosity and trapped in a web of responsibilities almost too great to fathom.

This is the only way I can sort through it—through my codes and my journals. I have no one to confide in and even if I did, I don't know that I could share this.

My mother's Lupus is getting worse by the day. She gets weaker and more depressed. My father is helpless. He's behind bars, and even his own family has turned against him. I am all he has, too!

I wish I knew a man strong, wise, and gentle enough to share all this with; but for now, and perhaps forever, I must be wise, strong, and compassionate.

I will succeed at this and everything for which I take responsibility. So, for now: Goodbye to *me*.

"Lollypop taste so sweet, you gotta lick the rapper."

I was chosen as the lead girl for a Lil Wayne video shoot. He took a liking to me right away and spent the entire day flirting and making comments about how attractive I was. At the end of the shoot, he hurried over before I could leave and asked me out and for my phone number.

"I'm sorry. But I have a boyfriend and too many people have my number already," I responded politely.

A few days passed and I got a call from my agent about a booking for a modeling shoot in Amsterdam for Young Money Records. The group was touring and they needed eye candy to be a part of the entourage, wear T-shirts, and hand out lollypops. This was one of those times when it just struck me (not that I'm ungrateful for my success) that we girls who do this are really just like wallpaper, window dressing, the bows on the gifts. However, as usual, I would get paid my daily rate plus all expenses, and a travel bonus because it was a long trip. I decided I wanted Dayane to join me for the fun we could have together. I told another of my agents that she spoke no English and until she became more acclimated to the U.S. I had to take her with me. I couldn't leave her alone in California.

He agreed and as an unexpected surprise, said Dayane would only get half of my rate. *Wow!* I hadn't been thinking about her getting paid; just getting her there would have been fantastic! When I told her she was not only going to Amsterdam, but she was also going to get paid, she nearly fainted! Although she's beautiful, she'd certainly never considered modeling, and then to get paid on top of that—well, it was almost too much for her to comprehend.

Our flight was from LAX to JFK and then on a private jet to Amsterdam. I had assumed (something I never do anymore) that the two of us would be flying alone. However, that was not to be because when we were seated, the pilot told us he had to wait for more passengers. Technically, the plane sat eight but, comfortably, really only six.

Twenty minutes later, Lil Wayne showed up with four other guys. I thought there would be other models but he told me they were flying commercial. This plane was reserved for me. I almost began to feel privileged, but my instincts told me this was not for my comfort, but Wayne's way of getting closer to me.

We touched down in Amsterdam nine hours later. During most of the flight, Wayne was rapping and putting together lyrics, while making a few indirect comments to me. He was about as subtle as an anvil.

Dayane and I spent most of our time ignoring him and his "boys." Giggling, we spoke in Portuguese, which irritated him, but I didn't care.

The minute we arrived, the flashbulbs started going off. There was a camera crew taping the behind-the-scenes parts for later possible use in the video. We hadn't even left the terminal before being told that we had to do interviews. There were six other models that joined us; some spoke English, others didn't. We weren't able to check into our rooms until later that evening, which made for a very long day.

I was given a key so that Dayane and I could go up to our room. I was surprised when we got there because the entry included an immense set of double doors: It was the Presidential Suite! The room was so extravagant that we both took pictures with our phones. There were three bedrooms, a giant kitchen and bar, living room, TV room, dining room, and three bathrooms.

"Are you sure this is our room?" Dayane asked.

"I guess, but I don't know why there are three bedrooms," I replied, just as perplexed.

Since we were both very tired, we chose our rooms and got ready for bed. The shooting would start early the next day. As we were unpacking, Lil Wayne walked in with his right hand man, Fuzz. I was confused and a little irritated that he could (and did) just walk into our suite but when I saw the expressions on their faces, I connected the dots.

"Now I understand why we're in the Presidential Suite," I said with my hands on my hips, throwing a little attitude into my voice. "We aren't comfortable sharing our rooms," I added.

Lil Wayne laughed. "We're all grownups here. This is the best room in the hotel and besides, there aren't any other rooms available. You two girls have your own rooms with locks. There shouldn't be any problems."

Thinking about it, I looked at Dayane and then back to Lil Wayne.

"Hey, it's not like we're all going to share one bed," Wayne said, and then the two men started laughing and I could smell weed on them as a bit of smoke escaped their mouths.

I told Dayane to grab her things. We were going to share one of the bedrooms, which we did, quickly falling asleep after securely locking the door.

Although Amsterdam is usually overcast, the sun poured through the window the next morning. After getting ready, Dayane and I went out to the living room, where we saw a huge breakfast—almost like a buffet—waiting for us. A chef was just finishing setting it up. Everything you could possibly think of was available: huge Belgian waffles, omelets of every description, potatoes, fruit, rolls, and things I didn't even recognize, primarily because my mind was still on our accommodations, locks or not.

Suddenly, there was a knock at the door. It was Fuzz telling us the bus was ready and that we had 45 minutes to make a one-hour ride to our location, so we grabbed our things and left without eating. I hoped all of that beautiful food would find its way to the staff.

That day, we went to five coffee shops for interviews and pictures. There were eight of us, and we all had to wear the silly T-shirts that read: "Licked the rapper," which came from a verse in one of his hits, "Lollypop," as in "Lollypop taste so good, you gotta lick the wrapper." We also had to hold large lollypops, act sexy, and smile a lot.

After the day's interviews, we went to a concert. On the way back to the hotel, I spoke with Lil Wayne. "Wayne, I'm still not comfortable. It's nothing about you personally. I just think we should have our own room, and we don't need anything so large."

Since he'd made passes at me all day, this didn't sit well with him. In fact, he became angry and raised his voice, saying, "What's the problem? Am I not your type?"

Not one to mince words at this point in my career, if ever for that matter, I replied, "No, you're not, and I'm trying to be a professional here. I'm trying to do my job. Isn't that what you hired me for?" I asked sarcastically.

This escalated into a full-blown argument at the end of which I said, "Fine. Then maybe it's best that Dayane and I leave."

"I can arrange that. I'll set up your travel," he answered, turning and storming out.

Since she didn't speak English, Dayane was dying to know what was said but I didn't tell her until we were back in our room.

Lil Wayne came back later that afternoon saying it had been too late to get in touch with the travel people and that he would take care of it the next morning.

I sighed.

"Look, why don't you sit down, have a toke and a drink, and relax?" he said, glancing at the couch next to him.

"No thanks," I said and went back to my room, leaving Dayane sitting across the coffee table from him. When I returned, she was smoking weed with Lil Wayne and Fuzz. I couldn't believe it. Yelling at her in Portuguese, I said, "What are you doing? I go take a shower and come back and you're hanging out with these two idiots?"

"I'm sorry, Sue," she said poutingly. "I was going to get some water when they offered me some weed instead. I thought it was cool. I've never tried it."

I was very disappointed and told her to go to our room. When she was gone, I read Wayne the riot act. "How dare you give my cousin drugs!"

"You know what, little diva? You have a real 'tude."

"You know what?" I argued back. "You're a jerk, and your nasty."

"Hey, fuck you. I'm gonna call my people tomorrow and have you taken out of all the videos."

"Thank you. I wouldn't want to be seen with you anyway, you pig."

All the while this was going on, I was thinking, *I get paid regardless.*

In the morning, Fuzz knocked on our door announcing that the limo was waiting and that the flight back was in two hours. After boarding the plane, we were whisked off on a commercial flight, flying home in coach class.

I assumed I would hear rumors or comments attributable to Wayne in the coming days and weeks, but instead, months later, rumors were circulating in the opposite direction about how I'd slept with him in Amsterdam.

As my career continued, I learned that 90-percent of what you read or hear about celebrities or Hollywood people is untrue. I would continue to read horrible lies about myself, which I guess I always will. I learned quickly to ignore it all, knowing I couldn't control any of it. Even though you have to grow a tough skin, I'm not complaining because I am grateful for all I've been given. I've also done well to choose the right assignments and people with whom I associate and know from experience how to keep the nasty parts at a minimum.

CAIRO

T O A NEWCOMER LIKE me, the streets of Cairo are a cacophony of stress: horns blaring nonstop, drivers seemingly in a perpetual rage, street vendors hawking their wares, cars whizzing back and forth between each other without benefit of any painted lines, pedestrians adept at dodging, and so forth. Sometimes a driver would either graze or slam into another car and then just continue on his way.

I was in the country with Anthony Parmonelle for a photo shoot for a print campaign for an appropriate advertiser, Sahara Clothing. I'd already been warned about the rules for women: no revealing clothes, cannot show skin, etc., etc. I love to travel and experience different people, places, and cultures, so I was very excited. While there, I 20-questioned everyone about everything every chance I got.

Our first day of shooting used the Pyramids as a set or backdrop, but getting out of the city in our car was daunting. After hours of driving in the desert, we made a stop by the Nile River where our guide and translator gave me a quick history lesson.

Back in the car, my stylists were working on my hair and make-up while I sat, absorbing all the sights: the small villages and the camels (which I'd never seen before). Suddenly, off in the distance, behind a two-story brick building, I could see the tip of a Pyramid. Driving closer, the Pyramids became larger and larger. I was amazed! When I asked why they weren't covered in gold, our translator laughed uncontrollably.

In another few moments, we were stopped at a gate where a guard looked at all of our passports, wrote down our names, and then allowed us through. A minute later, we were surrounded by the vast Egyptian desert and the Pyramids. It was surreal and awesomely beautiful.

My first outfit looked as if it were made of gold. The bra-style top was covered in gold beads, and I wore a stunning headpiece with a studded design, much like what an Egyptian goddess would have worn. The fitted skirt was similar to the top with hundreds of golden beads. My makeup was Cleopatra inspired with long black eyeliner tails that surrounded my eyes and went up, almost to my forehead.

After an hour of work, a giant plume of dust and sand began to appear off in the distance. I was in a van, which suddenly stopped so that six Egyptian men could jump out, three of them armed with automatic weapons. Our translator spoke with them, but then something I thought was routine turned horrific. The men grabbed us, pushing us into the back of the van, and then sped off. One of the armed men had commandeered our van with all of our props, makeup, clothes, and other belongings following behind us.

Frightened, I asked the translator what was happening, wanting to know where they were taking us.

She answered simply, "I do not know. They say we've disrespected the gods."

That did not sound good to me.

"Are they going to kill us?" the makeup girl wanted to know through her sobs.

The translator replied, "No. Just remain calm."

After another hour, the van stopped and a guard opened the back doors, pulling us out one by one. We were marched into a cold concrete room and told to form a line and then sit on the floor. The room looked a lot like the ones they use to torture people in the movies—dark gray concrete floor and walls, no windows.

I had to admit, at least to myself, that I was now petrified. As I sat on the floor in this incredible gold outfit, awaiting our fate, I envisioned myself languishing in jail, never seeing the light of day again, shriveling up to be a mere withered version of myself.

We remained there for three hours without water. The heavy steel door finally creaked open and a man in uniform stepped inside.

He spoke very little English, but his expression said volumes. He began to speak in Arabic. Our girl translated: "You have offended us. You were doing unbelievable things in front of our Pyramids. You have disrespected the gods."

Anthony spoke up, "Sir, with all due respect, we have permits to photograph here. We are shooting an advertising campaign for Sahara Clothing."

The translator interpreted and then the man became even angrier, yelling, "You call what she wears clothing?" pointing to me. "We will not allow pornography to be recorded here."

The man then turned, shouted an order to his guards, and they all walked out. *Did Anthony say the wrong thing? Were they going to keep us in prison, hang us, or what?*

A few more hours went by after the uniformed man and his guards left. Still without water, and all scared to death, speculation ran rampant within the group.

Before the sun was about to set, the door opened again and a different man entered, saying, "You may go. We have deleted all your material. You are not welcome here. Do not ever come back." With that, he dropped the cameras on the concrete floor than walked out, leaving the door open behind him.

As we drove back through the Pyramids to the hotel, a guard yelled in broken English, "We will remember your faces!"

A DIFFERENT KIND OF
AFRICAN TRIP

I WAS ABOUT TO LEAVE the house for lunch when the phone rang; it was one of my agents.

"Suelyn, I have a fabulous shoot for you. It's in Africa and it pays twenty grand."

I loved traveling and except for being thrown in a desert jail, Egypt was great fun. I love to fly. I love staying in nice hotels and, of course, I love modeling. I was also thinking about how much the money would help my family—a very nice shot in the arm.

"Book it, Dano," I said.

The next day she called back to let me know the shoot was in Nigeria.

I said, "Nigeria. Why Nigeria?"

"Because it's for Ariaka Airlines," she explained, "and that's where they want to shoot. Something to do with the backdrop, the owner, or both. I've never worked with this company. In fact, I've never heard of Ariaka Airlines, but we've checked them out and they're legit."

I said it was okay, albeit a little hesitantly. The agent had always been good to me, and she was smart. So, on the long trek, my first stop from Los Angeles was New York. There, I was to meet someone who would have a Nigerian visa ready for me. I thought it odd that I didn't have to go to the consulate, but I was assured the client had taken care of everything.

Traveling alone, at LAX, I boarded an Ariaka Airlines 747 and have to admit, I was very impressed. The plane was spectacular and had the best-looking first class lounge I'd ever been in, complete with an area where you could stand at the bar. On top of that, there wasn't anyone else in first class, so I had my pick of seats. In fact, there were very few people onboard at all. As I glanced behind me, the economy seats looked like a ghost town with only an occasional head poking up here and there.

It was a long flight and when I stepped out of the comfort of the air-conditioned first-class section of the aircraft, I felt like I was in Biloxi, Mississippi, in August, stepping into a wet blast furnace. The thermometer on the building at the airport read 102 degrees, and I knew the humidity was close to 95-percent. I was dripping wet before I got even three steps off the plane.

My next stop was at Customs. An apparent unhappy agent took one look at me and said, "What are you doing in Nigeria?"

"I'm here for a photo shoot for Ariaka Airlines."

"Where is your invitation?"

"Oh, you mean this?" I said, unfolding a letter I'd been given.

She looked at it, hummed a little, then grabbed the passport out of my hand, almost ripping out some of its pages. "You travel a lot," she said.

"Yes, I do. I'm fortunate enough to have a nice job that involves traveling."

"Where is your vaccine card?" she asked.

"I wasn't told I would need one."

"You can't go through without one. I don't care what they told you, whoever 'they' is," she said angrily.

"Well, I don't have one. I'll have to call my agent," I told her as I stepped out of line. By now, I was sweating as if I'd run a marathon in Palm Springs during the summer.

I couldn't get through to my agent on my cellphone, but I did have the number of a local contact by the name of Tula, in case I had any problems. I found a pay phone and called her but not before I first went to a currency exchange window. I'm not sure I got the right amount, and I didn't know which coins to use, so I just guessed. The first two coins didn't do the trick. Neither did the next two. *Geez*, I thought, *are these Nigerian pennies or is a local call just real expensive?* Eventually, I got Tula on the line and explained what happened.

She was in disbelief. "Give me a few minutes. I will come in and get you," she said.

Apparently, she'd been sitting out front waiting for me. I walked back to Customs and was about to tell the angry agent that my ride was about to clear everything up when in walked Tula and three security guards. As they approached my booth, she greeted me with, "Hello. I'm Tula, and I'm so *very* sorry for this matter."

With that, she turned abruptly and had the guards whisk the Customs' agent out to another room. Then, she turned, took my arm, and said, "Come on *Shoe-lin*," which is how she pronounced my name. "We have work to do."

Sensing trouble, I asked Tula, "What are they going to do with her?"

Without looking at me, and with my arm still in her hand, she responded, "She will get what she deserves."

Wow! I didn't know what to say. Even though the woman had been rude, I still felt bad nonetheless.

"She treated you with disrespect. You are a special invited guest here by the Prince. Do not trouble yourself about her."

"The Prince?"

"Yes, he is the owner of the airline as well as pretty much everything else in Nigeria. Shoe-lin, you are light skinned and beautiful. The women here will envy you. The Customs agent was jealous. She wanted to keep you from entering. She will get what she deserves."

At that point, I wasn't sure if this guy was the real Prince, or if that was his name. Whichever, he seemed to wield a lot of power. I began to wonder what I'd gotten myself into. Suddenly, twenty grand didn't look so great. God knows where I would be doing the shoot and in the heat, all I could hope for was that it was indoors; but, of course, I knew that wasn't going to be the case. *We could have done an indoor shot anywhere. Why fly for 14 hours to Nigeria?*

We drove for over an hour. Suddenly and literally, in the middle of nowhere, stood two massive white gates, as if Heaven were set in an African desert. There, behind the pearly white gates, back at the edge of a long road, stood an immense building, almost like a five-star hotel, which Tula explained was, in fact, a villa.

She showed me to the casitas where I would be staying. She gave me a cellphone, which she had already programmed to include her as the only contact on the phone.

"Today is your rest day, Shoe-lin. I'm sure you're weary from your long journey. When you are hungry or need *anything* (she emphasized that word), call me, or, if I'm not available, ask for Asa," who, at that precise moment, magically appeared.

I was very hungry (I hate airplane food regardless of how nice the plane is) so, Asa, a young woman, made dinner for me. When I sat down at the large table in the dining area, the meal looked delicious—a mixture of what appeared to be chicken, rice, and various vegetables. It looked and smelled so good, I quickly picked up my fork and began to eat, which lasted all of about five seconds before a searing heat enveloped my tongue, the roof of my mouth, and my throat. I had never eaten anything quite that spicy—in fact, spicy doesn't even begin to minutely describe the pain.

I couldn't stop coughing. I felt as though I had been poisoned and that I was choking to death. I dipped my napkin in the ice water and doused my mouth, which didn't help. In fact, if anything, it made it worse.

I'd heard about habama chilies, which are supposed to be half a million BTUs, but this was worse. Asa ran into the kitchen and brought me more water and a wet towel.

"Ms. Suelyn, I made it very light spicy like you requested," she said, afraid I was going to die on her watch.

I thought: *If this is the light, the regular must be like a bonfire*, but I didn't say anything negative. I just tried to smile as I said, "Asa, it's okay. I think a piece of food just went into my windpipe. I'll be alright."

I wanted to be very careful not to offend anyone. I'd traveled enough and seen a number of different cultures to know how things can be misinterpreted. What is polite in one country is disrespectful in another.

When Asa returned to the kitchen, I took my napkin and wiped as much of the red sauce off the chicken as I could so that I could manage to eat a little more.

It took an hour-and-a-half for the heat to subside. Before I went to bed, I looked at my tongue in the mirror to find that it was bright red and swollen like a hot sausage. Then I began to think about my stomach. *Will I awaken in the middle of the night and have to make a beeline to the bathroom, ending up there for the rest of the night? Will I get enough sleep so that I don't look like an old handbag in the morning?* Time would tell and there was no Pepto-Bismol in the medicine cabinet. In fact, there was nothing in the medicine cabinet.

Note to journal: *Make sure you always travel with a first-aid kit, and include plenty of Pepto!*

Early the next morning, Tula awakened me. Luckily, I'd made it through the night, managing to get about five hours of sound sleep.

"Good morning, Shoe-lin. The Prince would like to talk with you after you get dressed. He'd like to meet you, of course, and talk about the photo shoot."

"Great," I said. "What should I wear?"

I'd brought every conceivable outfit I could think (aka: Like a Good Girl, Be Prepared).

"Just stay away from any bright colors or anything revealing."

Well, she just ruled out nearly everything in my closet. However, being prepared for just about anything sartorial, I had packed some loose dresses, dark tops, and a bunch of cover-ups. I would also keep my face very clean and neutral, without too much makeup.

Before she closed the door, she said, "Oh, it's a long drive, so bring your book."

I thought, *My book? Does she mean something for me to read, or my portfolio?*

Sensing my dilemma, she pointed to the book on the bed that I'd read to go to sleep the night before.

I got dressed and then Tula escorted me to a room that was like a private waiting area in an office. All of the furniture was white with a significant amount of gold-leaf embellishments. Tula gestured for me to sit on the white couch. Everything in the room seemed to be decorated with gold, including the glass coffee table in front of the couch. On the table were also about 20 magazines spread out, with stacks of more of them on the edge of the table.

As I began to hunt through them, I was surprised to see that they all had my picture on the cover—some of which I didn't even have copies!

I pulled out my cellphone to take a picture; otherwise, my friends wouldn't believe it. Then, as I scanned the waiting room, I saw one of my calendars on the far wall. It was the month of October, which I didn't understand because it was now April.

I was taking all this in when a polite young woman came in and offered me tea. When she brought it to me, I pretended to take a sip, and then placed it on the table. I have a rule: I only drink from closed bottles (like water bottles) unless I'm in my own home; I never drink from a glass or cup.

I left the tea on the table and within a couple of minutes, the Prince entered the room. (At least I assumed he was the Prince.) He seemed a little nervous but was trying not to show it.

"Hello, Suelyn. I'm T, Prince T. Not like the tea you're drinking, just the letter T."

I said, "Okay," and smiled.

Prince T sat in a large white chair in front of me, across from the coffee table. He started right in without any other small talk, first mentioning his airline and then some other companies he owned. Then we began to talk more thoroughly about the airline.

"I have an idea for a commercial," he started. We discussed his idea when he abruptly stopped and changed the subject.

"Were you born in Brazil?" he asked.

"No. I was born in New York, but my parents are Brazilian and I spent a great deal of time there with my grandparents and parents, on and off."

T responded to this in Portuguese. I did likewise. He said he loved Brazil; I, in turn, said I was there for the Carnival last year and had a Camarinho booth at the Beija Flor.

During the Carnival, there's a big competition where teams from different cities compete. They work all year preparing costumes, songs, and dances, then at the Carnival, they display their acts and the best one wins.

"Beija Flor was my team from Rio," I told him.

"Fascinating," he said with genuine interest.

Using a few words of French, he then launched into how he was born in Africa but raised in Paris. After a few moments of his history, he stood and said, "Do you mind if I have a drink?"

Hey, it's your house, I wanted to say. "No, of course not," at which point he walked over to a large armoire-type cabinet, opened it, and displayed about 30 bottles of different kinds of liquor. He poured himself a healthy scotch and then sat again after taking a large gulp, apparently to calm his nerves a bit.

"Suelyn, I am fascinated with your work."

"Thank you. I noticed you have a number of my magazines," I said, glancing at the display on the coffee table.

"It wasn't easy collecting them all but I wanted to make sure I had every copy in which you've appeared."

His comment made me squirm ever so slightly, but then I figured that he was just another fan who also happened to be a billionaire.

"I noticed you have my calendar as well, but it's set to the wrong month. Let me fix it for you," I offered, standing so I could do so.

"No," he said quickly. "I have it set to April for a reason. Because that is my birthday month, I would like you to autograph it." He handed me a pen and I signed it with a flourish. As I finished, I turned and asked, "Are we shooting anything in particular today?"

"No. I have everything set up for tomorrow," he quickly answered.

"Oh? Well, that might be a problem because I have a flight back to New York tomorrow night."

"Suelyn, you forget. I own the airline. You can leave whenever I want you to do so."

I was trying to be more than polite, but his tone sounded a little ominous. *"Whenever* he *wanted me to do so"?*

Before he left, I said, "T, I have obligations in Los Angeles this weekend on both Saturday and Sunday—a shoot for a hair commercial for Top Styler and another for *944 Magazine.*

His only response was a very abrupt, "Oh, that's nice. I'll see you tomorrow," and then he was gone.

Tula was waiting for me outside the door. On the way back to my casitas, she said, "Well, what do you think of him?"

"He's certainly a gentleman."

"He definitely likes you."

"Why do you say that?" I had to ask. "He does apparently like my work because I saw the magazines and the calendar."

Tula laughed but didn't say anything more. Then her phone rang. She flipped it open and said, "Yes, sir. Okay. One moment, sir," and handed the phone to me. "Prince T wishes to speak with you."

"Hello."

"Hello, Suelyn. I would like to invite you to have dinner with me tonight."

"Oh, thank you; that would be great but I have to prepare for tomorrow's shoot. I want to make sure my hair and nails are just right You know—model stuff, girl stuff."

"Have dinner with me and my friends. There will be plenty of time to prepare tomorrow," he said more like an emphatic command rather than a suggestion. I was beginning to get the gist of what was happening. My thoughts were: *This guy is wealthy beyond belief. He can afford "anything," and his anything now is me. He's managed to get me here using a photo shoot as a pretext for us to "get to know one another."* His ploy wasn't much different than the one I wrote about earlier in this book with the various photographers, Pastors, etc.

There I was, metaphorically speaking, driving down the 405 Freeway with a sign in front of me that read, "Construction Detour Ahead." I needed to get off at Santa Monica Boulevard, way before the congestion, or in this case, the problem.

However, I didn't want to be rude and I couldn't absolutely be positive that was his game plan, or at least a portion of it.

"Okay, then dinner it is," I told him, still wondering how I would back out, using my fake excuse of the two L.A. shoots.

I was ready at 6:00 p.m. Asa entered my casitas and said, "The car is out front," and then she walked with me and opened the enormous doors. Sitting in the driveway was a blue and silver Bugatti. One of its doors opened and T stepped out, "You look ravishing, my dear," he said, putting an arm around me as he escorted me to the other side of the car, opening the door for me.

Oh my. What have I gotten myself into? I am in a very strange, very distant country with a man I know absolutely nothing about, other than that he was supposedly "the client."

As he drove, he showed me all the things the car could do while pressing all kinds of buttons on the dashboard. I had been in just about every luxury car you can name, and this one really took the cake, but I didn't want to act amazed or too impressed.

"So, your friends are meeting us for dinner?" I asked.

"Oh. I forgot to tell you. They were detained. We'll be dining alone."

Oh boy!

Within about 20 minutes, we arrived at a set of gates even higher than the ones at the villa. Two armed men were standing on either side as we entered. I knew I was in trouble, but I also knew we'd already passed Santa Monica Boulevard.

I had to think clearly before saying anything else. Somehow, without angering him, I had to tell him that I wasn't interested in anything but the photo shoot—that I was a professional, here to do a job. At this point, I was way past worrying about being polite.

While I was thinking about how I would say what I had to say, we pulled into the world's largest private garage. I was stunned! There were at least a hundred cars lined up in many rows, one after another after another. What made the visual even more surreal was the fact that every one of them was either blue, silver, or white, and, except for the white, the others were the exact same shade of blue and silver.

After opening my door, T gestured that I should follow him. As my now self-appointed tour guide, he showed me the McLarens, Ferraris, Lamberginis, Rolls Royces, Bugattis, Mercedes, and many others I didn't recognize.

He was beaming like a little boy, proudly showing off his complete collection of GI Joe soldier figures.

"How do you like my collection?"

"They're beautiful. You have great taste."

"Which one would you like to test drive?" he asked seriously. "I have read in magazine interviews that you love to drive fast cars."

That was the instant that I knew he was a stalker. He must have read every interview ever published about me. Worse yet, he thought he knew me based on what he'd read. As the goose bumps started running up and down my arms, I could feel my stomach begin to twitch. However, no matter how much I was creeped out, I had to stay focused.

"That's okay. I think they're all fantastic, but I'm not really dressed for it—you know, to really let it loose."

That didn't sit well with him. I could see his expression change instantly.

"Pick one or I will," he said emphatically, and then he pressed a small remote he'd had in his pocket and a door opened in the back of the garage, revealing a complete racetrack. I felt like I was in a movie about a giant who has all these little toys, ready to play with, everything laid out like in real life, only all in one place—just a fingertip command away.

"Dinner won't be ready for an hour, so we have time. Let's have some fun and test ride some of these machines," he said, now smiling again. "I'm going to have a drink. Can I make you one?"

Pushing the remote again, a wet bar popped up from the floor, this one filled with every kind of liquor imaginable. Even though I drink very little, and then only in a social setting, I walked over without hesitation, grabbing the Patron.

"I'll have a shot of this," I said, grabbing a Dixie cup—the safest receptacle I could find at the bar.

He chose a McLaren. Because I couldn't believe he was really going to let me drive one of his cars, I chose one of the Bugattis, which he showed me how to start. When I was in his other Bugatti, because it had so many toys, bells, and whistles, I had carefully observed everything he did.

When both cars were warmed up, I ever so gingerly eased the Bugatti out of the garage. The floor was either polished concrete or some sort of exotic marble because it was polished to a shine that rivaled any nail job I'd ever had. The tires squeaked as we moved slowly through the big back door, past the rows and rows of other exotic vehicles.

Once on the track, I started slow, increasing speed a little more after each lap. He was close behind. The track was probably a mile long and had lots of twists and turns, but none too dangerous.

After about 20 minutes, he said, "Let's drive some others." I chose the Ferrari F 430 this time, the one like Peter gave me to drive. When it was finally time for dinner, we parked the cars in their designated spots. Each of which had a name painted on it.

From the garage, we entered the villa from a side door, and I found myself in an enormous dining room with a table that seated probably 50 people. Only two places were set—side-by-side.

He pulled out my chair for me and sat down.

"T, I have something to say to you."

"Yes, please go ahead. You may speak freely."

"First, thank you for the lovely accommodations. Thank you, too, for letting me drive your incredible cars and, finally, thank you for treating me like a queen. However, I must tell you that I am not interested in anything but doing my job: doing the shoot and then going home." I paused. He didn't say anything, so I continued.

"I just want you to know—no, I need you to know—that if you have any other intentions, I am not interested. I have a loving relationship at home and I never stray. I also don't mix my business with my personal life. This has already gone further than with what I'm comfortable."

He looked chagrined, genuinely surprised, and maybe even a little hurt.

"Suelyn, I just wanted you to have dinner with me. I knew you liked fast cars so I thought you might enjoy driving a couple of them. That's all; nothing else."

I didn't believe him, but I smiled and told him I appreciated his kindness. Given his stature, it seemed a little too convenient that his friends had been indisposed at the last second. The collection of magazines bothered me and, as if she knew very well what I was in for, even Tula's laugh was a little disconcerting.

From that point until he took me back to my casitas, he was a perfect gentleman and, since I'm sure they'd gotten word from Asa about the spices, the food was excellent. However, I knew he was waiting for the right moment.

When I returned to my casitas, I called one of my agents on the global phone Tula had given me. I explained things weren't what they might have seemed. I was scheduled for the next day's shoot and didn't think I'd make it back in time for the L.A. work over the weekend. I also told her I didn't feel safe.

There was silence for a moment and then she said, "Suelyn, he didn't make a pass at you, and he hasn't touched you. Just complete the shoot and I'll make sure you are on the first flight out after you're finished."

I liked this agent. She was a good person. But at the end of the day, agents have to make a living, too; that's what they do. They get 20-percent of your wages, but they don't get anything if you screw up or don't show up.

The next morning, Tula awakened me for an 8:00 a.m. departure.

"Shoe-lin, I'm going to drop you off at the plane, so bring the clothes you wish," she said.

Huh?

"The shoot is going to be on the plane. Bring any personal items you want."

Well, I guess that made sense. I had no script and no idea of what T wanted to do, but I packed everything I thought I'd need.

We arrived an hour later at the same airport but, this time, they took me through some back gates to a smaller white plane. Once I'd pulled my case out, Tula said, "Okay. Goodbye. Enjoy," and that was that; she was gone. I stood alone on the tarmac, wondering what would happen next.

Finally, a man in a white uniform (so much white everywhere) approached me. He told me he would take my things and asked me to follow him to the white jet. Once we were onboard, I asked him if this was where we would be shooting. He replied, "I don't know. Ask T when he gets here."

The plum-colored carpets were plush, much more so than any home carpet I'd ever stepped on; the padding alone must have been three inches thick.

I glanced around the incredible plane. It was the most customized aircraft I'd ever seen.

As I was doing my make-up, T came aboard. He greeted me and began to share the plan of the day, starting with, "We will land at a location . . ."

Whoa! Now we're flying somewhere else?

"We will be shooting on this plane and also on the Ariaka plane on which you first arrived," he explained. "And now, finally, here is my idea," he began. "You will be filmed flying in this plane, my G-4, and also in the Ariaka airliner. You will find flying in the airliner just as nice as this G-4. Get it?" he said gleefully and very proudly.

I concurred.

Then he pulled open a briefcase. Inside was an amazing jewelry collection, including the biggest diamonds I'd ever seen.

"I'm saving these for my princess," he said, smiling.

I guess my look gave away my *sure you are* thought.

"No, really. I am looking for a princess."

That was the end of that conversation. We settled in, buckled our seat belts, and flew for over an hour. According to T, the G-4 could fly unfettered at about 650 miles per hour, and even more if he wanted, so that meant we were about 600 miles away from his villa (and I didn't even know if we were still in Nigeria).

Wherever we landed, it was gorgeous. When we touched down, a crew was waiting for us and the Ariaka Airlines plane was sitting nearby. So far, so good.

The shoot lasted hours, most of which was in the interior of both planes. Outside, the heat index was brutal. T seemed happy with the results the director showed him. As far as I was concerned, I was done and couldn't stop thinking about the 18-hour flight home. Fourteen hours to New York and then on to L.A. However, I had no idea what was supposed to happen next. T knew I needed to leave that night. Yet, he turned to me and said, "Would you like to go to Cape Town? It's only an hour from here."

"I'm sorry, T. I really can't. Like I said, I have two jobs I have to complete in L.A."

"Okay. I understand."

Whew!

The flight back was silent. When we arrived at the airport, before I could get my things out, T pushed a button and the privacy window between the driver and us came up. We were now alone.

"Suelyn, you did a wonderful job out there today. The commercial is going to be a big success," and I'm thinking, *Why in the world did we have to fly out to nowhere for an hour, when all the shots were inside the two planes that could have been sitting at this airport?*

"I have a gift for you," he said.

"Oh no. I can't accept any gifts. You don't need to do that."

"Well, if you won't take it as a gift, then please just wear it in L.A., since you'll be modeling my line." Having said that, he pulled out a blue-velvet-lined box, which he opened. Inside was a stunning canary-yellow diamond necklace. The yellow diamonds, with white ones surrounding them, were quite large. It was exquisite.

"Oh my," I said. "This takes my breath away," which it did. "Thank you, but I can't accept such a gift."

"It's not polite to reject a gift from a Prince, you know. It's yours."

The tone of his voice—almost a threat—suggested that I had no choice, so I said, "Okay. It is very lovely. Thank you very much. I will wear it in L.A."

"I am leaving in the morning for South Africa for some business. It was a pleasure meeting and working with you. I hope you have a safe journey home," T said graciously.

The car stopped in front of the casitas where I was staying. I got out, said my goodbyes, and started to go inside when I heard his window go down.

"Suelyn, wait. You forgot your box."

"Oh, I'm so sorry," I said, going back to the car. He handed the box to me and then placed his hand on top of mine. "Here is my private cell number. Don't lose it. You may want it if you change your mind," he said.

God, they never give up, no matter how many times or however politely I say NO.

Needless to say, I didn't leave that night. The next morning, Tula told me that my flight had been scheduled for 9:00 p.m. that evening. I would gain about seven hours heading west, but I'd be exhausted when I got there.

Before she left, I said, "Tula, are there any orphanages around here?" I had researched the possibilities online and believed one to be close, but needed her to confirm my findings.

"Yes, Shoe-lin. There is the Arrows of God Orphanage not far away. Would you like me to schedule a visit for you?"

"Yes, please. Could we go in the next couple of hours?"

"Certainly, Ms. Shoe-lin."

A driver picked me up about an hour later; within minutes, I was inside the orphanage talking with the administrator. I asked her if they accepted donations, which, of course, they did. When she told me I could shop in their little store and drop off any donations there, I went back to the car where Tula was waiting and asked, "Can you take me to this address, please?"

Tula recognized it as the local market. I bought 10 large bags of rice and bags of cookies and sweets for delivery to the orphanage. Ms. Jane, the administrator was very thankful and insisted on giving me a certificate of some sort. "If you would like," she said, "I could also give you a tour of the classrooms."

Jumping at the chance, we immediately started to walk down a long hall with rooms on both sides. I believe the building was made of sandstone. It was almost adobe looking, resembling something in a poor neighborhood in Mexico

When we walked into the first room, it was filled with boys and girls from about 7 to 12 years of age. None of them wore shoes, and their clothing looked more like long-ago hand-me-downs, or even rags. I began to have one of my gut clenches when all of the kids thanked me in unison after Ms. Jane told them about my donation. I could see on every one of their faces how appreciative they were, how solemn and full of gratitude. As the tears began to well up in my eyes, it nearly broke my heart.

My mind started darting off in so many different directions: thoughts about my own behavior, money excesses, buying meaningless things I would never use. I looked at the children's feet. Most of them were either barefoot or wearing sandals made of strips of tire tread, which made me think of my closet back home with about 200 pairs of shoes in it. And then I thought about the yellow diamond necklace. The more I thought about all of this, the more I felt as though I was going to break down into a puddle of tears.

When some of the kids ran over and began hugging me, I nearly lost it. It's difficult now to explain the physical and spiritual feelings that ran through my mind—it was electrifying, yet sad at the same time. With the possible exception of when my mother, my sisters, and I distributed all those things in the slums of Rio, I had never experienced anything like it.

One of the little girls began touching my purse. Ms. Jane scolded her, telling her not to do so.

"It's okay," I said.

The little girl was persistent. Even though Ms. Jane was admonishing her, she dug her hand inside and then made a gesture with her finger across her lips several times. I knew immediately she wanted to use my lipstick.

"Come here, honey," I said, taking her over to a corner of the room away from the rest of the children. I took out my tube of red lipstick, opened it, and put it in her hand, closing it around the tube so no one could see. She ran off as excited as someone who had just won the lottery.

Driving back to the villa, Tula asked if I had enjoyed my visit. "Did you really like it, or were you just doing that for pictures?"

I was surprised and hurt. That had never occurred to me, but I also understood the question from her perspective.

"I didn't take any pictures, Tula. I would never do that."

"It's just that I never thought a model would go to such a place."

"Tula, being a model is not a definition of who I am; it's just my job."

I could sense that she felt defensive about having asked, so she quickly changed the subject.

"So, how did it go yesterday on your shoot?"

"It went well.

"The Prince didn't give you any gifts?" she asked.

"I don't understand your question, Tula."

Because she was acting very strange, I kept my bag close to me at all times.

In the morning, I wrapped the necklace in tissue paper and put it in the padding of my bra, which I then sewed closed. I didn't trust leaving it at the villa. I'd heard stories about Nigeria, all of which were very bad.

When I received the payment for the shoot in cash, I put it in the lining of my small suitcase, which is when Tula started talking about her "cut."

I was taken aback. "I don't know what kind of deal you might have made with my agent, Tula, but you'll have to take that up with her."

Not to be deterred, she countered, "Shoe-lin, I have served you faithfully. I have been a good friend to you. You must give me twenty percent."

I couldn't believe what I was hearing, so I merely said, "No."

"I know the Prince. He is a very generous man. He must have paid you well and also given you a nice gift."

"I'm not sure what you think he gave me other than payment for my work. I was *not* given any extra money."

"Shoe-lin, I can help you. You cannot leave the country with more than ten thousand dollars."

"Yes, I'm aware of that."

"I know you have more than that. If they find it on you at the airport, they will take everything—this is Nigeria. If you give me my twenty percent, I will make sure you get through without being checked."

"I don't know what you're talking about."

"All I want is my twenty percent, what I agreed to—the amount I am due."

"Tula, I didn't agree to anything with you. I have to pay my agent the same percentage. If she promised you something then that needs to come out of her share. I know nothing about any extra twenty percent."

"You don't understand Shoe-lin. Your agent promised me you would give me twenty percent. We knew you would get extra money from the Prince and I would get twenty percent."

"Hold on a minute. I never agreed to anything like this. I never heard about this, and I'm not paying you a dime."

"You are a liar. Your agent told me twenty percent for her and the same for me because I told her T would give you extra."

"So you and my agent set this up behind my back, without my knowledge?"

We continued arguing for several minutes, Tula telling me I was a liar and a thief, that I never would have gotten the job without her setting it up, so she was due her share.

"Tula, here is the long and the short of it. You aren't getting a nickel. Do you think I would fly for eighteen hours each way to this godforsaken shit hole, nearly have to fight off the Prince for three days, and spend one entire day in the hundred and three degree heat, to give you and her forty percent of what I made? That means, for all my work, time, and experience, I would end up with twelve thousand dollars! I can make that at home in L.A. in less than two hours."

"I don't care what you make or how. I don't even care what you did with the Prince. You owe me twenty percent and if you don't give it to me, you aren't going home. If I tip them off, they'll probably throw you in jail for smuggling. Can you imagine what the jails in Nigeria are like?"

I was exasperated. I walked out of the room and returned to my casitas to call my agent. It was now 4:00 p.m., and my flight was at 9:00 p.m. with a two-hour ride to the airport.

When I got my agent on the phone, I was practically in a rage. She proceeded to tell me she had, in fact, set up a deal with Tula; that Tula told her I'd be getting some very nice gifts or at least more money, which would make me happy. Everyone would win.

I was furious. "How could you pull a deal like this behind my back?" I screamed.

"How much did he give you?" she asked. I told her it was $20,000 as agreed.

"Suelyn, be honest with me."

"Honest with you!? How about you being honest with me? You never told me anything about this and now I might get thrown in jail. You work for me, not the other way around."

Now, I was really getting mad. How dare she put together a deal behind my back. How dare she accuse me of lying. How dare she put me in danger in this hole halfway around the world.

"Listen, sister, and listen good. You put me in this fucking mess. My flight leaves in a few hours, this woman is trying to rob me, and I might get either thrown in jail or killed. You will get your twenty percent when I return. Now get me the hell out of here. Call a driver or a cab or whatever, but I only have a few hours. I will deal with this bitch here."

I hung up the phone. I went back out to the living room and told Tula that my agent had agreed to deposit 20-percent into her account but I understood she would feel better getting it in cash now. "Here," I said, sticking my hand out with $4,000.

Instead of happily taking her ill-gotten gains, she started screaming, "I am not going to take this small amount of money. I know the Prince gave you more. You are lying."

That was it! I'd had it. I wanted to slap this woman so hard, her family would feel it.

"Okay. Then here is what I'm going to do. I'm going to call T and tell him everything that you have been saying and doing. I'm going to tell him that you are trying to extort twenty percent out of me. I cannot miss my flight, so either take the cash or suffer your own fate with T." Provided he wasn't in on it, I knew that she would be scared to death of him.

I packed the rest of my things and headed to the door, not knowing what I was going to do, just hoping she'd fall for the call to the Prince and it would scare her.

Tula was standing guard at the door when I told her, "Your money is on the bed. Take it or leave it. And, while you're at it, call me a cab."

"You are not leaving, miss high and mighty model girl."

"That's what you think. I've already called T. I told him that you and I had a little misunderstanding and I need a ride to the airport. I can call him back again if you like so I can tell him the rest."

I could tell *that* scared her and I'd been able to bluff my way out of a very bad poker hand.

She began to tremble at the thought of what T might do to her. At the very least, she would lose her cushy job. At worst—who knew? She promptly had a car come around, I put my things in it, and the three of us took off for the airport.

The drive took a little over two hours and when I finally got there, I'd missed the plane by 15 minutes, knowing Tula had taken some detour along the way to ensure that happened.

I was frantic! I asked the agent if there were any more international flights out tonight. There were none. When I asked about national flights, he said, "Yes. There is one. It goes to Lagos. It leaves in ten minutes."

Since I'd never even heard of Lagos, I didn't know where it was.

"Okay, give me a ticket to Lagos," I said.

After checking the bags to a different destination, I almost missed that flight, too.

When I finally arrived in Lagos, I got a hotel room. I would miss my next two photo shoots, but I'd be alive. As soon as I sat down on the bed, I called the private number T had given me and explained the whole story in detail. He was truly aghast. He couldn't believe it until I told him I was in a hotel in Lagos; I also told him I left the extortion money on the bed in the villa.

The next morning, T had a driver waiting to take me directly to the airport and through security. I was finally on my way back to L.A. It was a very long flight, made even longer each time I relived my nightmare in Nigeria.

The only business left to do was to fire my agent—face to face—and I couldn't wait to do so. I can't say what might have happened to Tula, but as she would have said herself, I'm sure, "She got what she deserved."

CHAPTER SEVEN

My Mother's Drug Habit

A FEW DAYS AFTER MY mother got out of the hospital for her Lupus treatments, I went back to New York for a visit. The holidays weren't far off. She was weak and tired, but she was managing fairly well with the help of her medications.

Since most of my mom's acquaintances were from the church, she'd made friends with a woman by the name of Paulina. One afternoon she said, "My friend, Paulina, is having a little get together and a poker party. Let's all go over there."

One of the problems with Lupus is the depression most patients go through. I figured my mother was just "down" and she wanted to have a little fun and play cards, so my sisters and I went with her to her friend's apartment that afternoon. There were several women there, all talking, listening to music, and playing cards. My sister, Evelyn's, boyfriend also came over.

After we'd been there for about half an hour, my mother told me she was going with Paulina to the store, which, under her circumstances, I didn't think was a good idea because I was always worried that, in her weakened state, she'd fall.

"What do you need?" I asked. "I'm not playing cards, so I can get it for you."

"No, no, Suelyn. That's okay. Paulina and I will go. It will only take a few minutes."

After they left, I went to the window. The apartment was on the second floor of a dingy old brick building in Queens, and I watched as they disappeared around the corner. As Mom had promised, they returned in about half an hour, both smiling but without any groceries or bags, which I thought was odd.

The card game continued. By this time, I'd joined in and was winning some change when my mother excused herself to go to the bathroom. As she walked down the hall, Paulina followed. They entered the bathroom together, closing the door behind them.

We all grew up casually in my family. We dressed around each other and never really closed a door. But if we did, a knock on the door was usually sufficient to gain entrance.

As I raked in another pile of penny chips, I began to wonder what was taking the women so long. After about fifteen minutes, curiosity got the best of me and I bowed out of the next hand, went down the hall, and knocked on the door.

"Hey, are you two okay in there?" I asked.

At first, it was silent. Then I heard the toilet flush.

"We'll be out in a minute, honey," my mother called. When I heard the toilet flush again, like a shockwave, it suddenly hit me. I knew what they were doing, but I couldn't bring myself to admit it to myself. *Can this be possible? My mother? It can't be!*

Finally, when the door slowly opened, Paulina came out with a sinister smile on her face and my mother remained inside. I pushed open the door further and said, "Mom, what's going on?"

"Nothing, dear. Nothing at all," she said nervously from where she stood at the sink. "Let me finish using the bathroom." I looked in her hand, which she was trying to hide behind her, to see that she was holding a Kotex pad.

"What's that for?" I asked incredulously.

"Oh, it's the oddest thing. I think my period is coming back."

Huh? At the age of 45?

She put the pad in her purse and wiped white residue from her nose, then stepped around me so she could return to the living room. Although I felt nauseous and emotionally side-blinded, I also felt this ache in my heart for her. She was my mother. She worked so hard and took care of my sisters and me. She loved and adored my father and had gone through so much, from poverty to moving back and forth, which seemed to be a regular thing, especially not having my father around.

In that moment, I saw the weakness in her that we never want to see in those we love, especially our parents. But it's always there. None of us is perfect, but I wanted to think that at least my mother wasn't so weak she'd resort to sniffing cocaine. But it wasn't to be because the look on her face as she wiped her nose was that of a little girl—just like me many years ago—a little girl who'd been caught with her hand in the cookie jar. Only, when she's not a little girl and she's your mother, it's not cute because it's so very, very sad.

I felt guilty for judging her. Guilt wrapped around disdain or monumental disappointment was enough to make me want to vomit—for both of us.

My mind raced back to earlier years when my parents sniffed cocaine at the parties they had. It even reminded me of that evil, vile worker who did that unspeakable thing to me when I was 7. I started thinking of all the people I knew at all the clubs and parties I'd gone to who did cocaine and other drugs. I started thinking of how much I hated the drug scene. My mind was reeling. That was the real reason I hated drugs because it all went back to when I was a child observing how stupid my parents acted—these two loving, bright, hard-working people sniffing powder up their noses and acting like they owned the world. I hated it!

I followed my mother down the hall, my disappointment in her almost unbearable. I was experiencing about four different horrible emotions at once. Of all the people in the world, my mother was doing drugs and just four days out of the hospital—and her church "friends" were her cohorts!

When I got back to the living room, her mood had changed completely. She was laughing and being silly, like a little girl. Where was my mother? Even though I wanted to break down and cry, and throw something heavy across the room, I also didn't want to alarm Evelyn and Raquel.

Trying to pull myself together, I returned to the bathroom, closed the door, and began to cry uncontrollably. After a few moments, listening to the women all joking and laughing, I realized they were all doing drugs. I wiped my eyes, splashed some cold water on my face, and went back out.

"Mom, Evelyn, Raquel—grab your stuff; we're leaving."

My mother looked surprised and even a little angry. "What? The fun is just starting."

"Mom, I want to go. We have to go right now." I raised my voice, "Mom, come on! We are leaving *now*." I looked at my sisters whose mouths were hanging open in surprise. "Come on," I said again.

Just then, my cellphone chirped. Looking down, I saw a text message from Evelyn, who had already worked her way out into the hallway. It simply said, "Oh, I guess you found out."

What? She knew and hadn't told me?

Then, behind the first text came another, "It's been going on for a long time."

Oh my God!

I went out into the hall, grabbed Evelyn's hand, and pulled her downstairs. "What are you talking about?"

"Mom has been doing this for a while, Suelyn. We didn't want to hurt you, because you have so much going on, so many problems already."

"I don't understand. I just don't understand."

"Suelyn, she gets like this. She parties and then she wakes up super depressed because she's mad at herself for doing it. Then she gets on the Christian thing again and goes to church every day and takes us along, where we have to sit in the pews with her, stare up at Jesus hanging from the cross, and watch as she prays for hours."

I hadn't a clue. Evelyn was 16 but not nearly as mature as I was at that age. All this time I kept thinking my sisters were just being rebellious, when it wasn't them at all. They were just responding to my mother's problems. They didn't know what to do, any more than I did.

At that moment, a bright light bulb went on over my head. I'd been so protective of them all these years, trying to keep them from danger—and here was a very real and serious danger right in their own home.

I'd been a full-time surrogate mom and now that I'd moved to California, I knew they really needed my help, but I wasn't there to give it.

I jerked myself out of my thoughts and the loud laughter from the living room came back to me. The women were joking, throwing cards on the table; and they'd turned up the music even louder.

"Mom! *Mom*, we're leaving! I've already put the girls in the car."

She looked sad, incredulous, and didn't move. I grabbed her bag and said, "Come on. We're leaving . . . *NOW!*"

Clearly upset, Paulina stood as if to block me. She had a very stern, I'm-old-enough-to-be-your-mother look on her face, which tempted me to punch her.

Since I was the one driving my mother's car that night, I took her by the hand, we went down to the car silently, got in, and I started driving home. From the backseat where she was sitting with Raquel, Mom said, "Suelyn, you're just no fun at all. It's still so early. Why do we have to go home?" By that time, she'd added fuel to the fire with all the wine she'd had. There is nothing quite so depressing as hearing a parent slur their words or watch them stumble around. I had never experienced it before and I didn't like it now.

As I continued to navigate the busy streets of Queens, my mother kept defending herself.

"Suelyn, you don't know what it's like. I had a very rough time in the hospital, and now it's time for me to have some fun." Her words were practically dripping from her mouth. "Why do we have to go home?"

Sitting at a red light, I was beginning to get angrier. When you're sober and people around you are stoned or inebriated, it's a very odd and not so nice feeling. You forget how powerful or smart or wise they seemed to be. Instead, all of a sudden, they are stupid, silly, powerless, and disgusting.

As mad as I was, I was also still fighting the many emotions I was experiencing. I knew I didn't want to say anything else to my mother in front of my sisters because that would be disrespectful.

After the long ride home, I told my sisters to go to their rooms, straight to bed. My mother meandered off to her room. Suddenly remembering that she still had drugs in her purse, I threw my own on the couch and followed her to her room to find her sitting on the edge of the bed, looking so forlorn. I didn't know what to say. *Should I wait until tomorrow when she's sober?*

I played dumb.

"Mom, what's going on. You weren't drinking in the bathroom. What were you doing in there?"

Still in denial, she answered, "What are you talking about? I can't even have a drink?"

Silently, I just stood in front of her, listening as she continued to blame my father's absence, the stress, her disease—everything was an excuse to remove herself from the harshness of her reality. I felt bad and angry at the same time.

"Mom. Stop talking about all of that! I know what our problems have been, but this is different. You don't need to use drugs to solve this."

"I don't know what you're talking about. Leave me alone," she sniffled, wiping her runny nose.

I gave up and left her room, hoping she would go to sleep. She certainly wasn't going anywhere, but I was worried she'd get into her purse again. I wanted time to think about how to talk with her when she was sober—as the oldest daughter, I was the mother now, which is never easy.

As I was sitting on the couch formulating a plan, I heard her open her door and come out into the living room. She had her keys and her purse.

"I'm going out to see Paulina," she said, as if nothing had happened. I looked down the hall to make sure the girls were in their rooms.

"Over my dead body," I said, standing up abruptly. I ran over to the door and stood in front of it. She tried to push me out of the way.

"I'm an adult," she said, slurring her words. "You can't tell me what to do. You've got our roles reversed here."

"You're *not* going anywhere, and I mean it, Mom." Then, I grabbed her keys and purse. I didn't think she'd put up a fight, but she tried to get the keys out of my jeans' pocket where I'd quickly shoved them. She continued to push at me, grabbing at my pocket. Knowing I was stronger, I grabbed her, dragging her down the hall to her room, while she continued to chatter and complain about being "the adult" and "the mother."

Mom had always been my friend, my *best* friend. This was just beyond my comprehension. I'd never seen her like this. As I pulled her into her room, thinking, *What am I going to do, tie her up?*, I heard the girls come out into the hall.

"Evelyn, please take Raquel into your room. I'm talking with Mom. Please just go. This is private."

They retreated just enough so that they thought I couldn't see them, but I knew they were there, not missing a second of what was happening. I was in a real mess. I didn't want the girls to witness this, but I had to control my mother. I wanted a magic solution, a brilliant last-second decision that would immediately fix this situation.

During this period of time, I'd been sending my mother money every week to help with the bills—plenty to get by on, and then some. How much of it had been going to drugs? I knew she and my father had a savings account, so I'd hoped the overflow was going there; but now she was telling me all the money was gone and, of course, telling me she hadn't spent it on drugs.

Although I was able to talk with my father every week in jail, he had to initiate the calls, which I could only get at my mother's place, so I had to wait.

When I did have conversations with him, he only wanted to catch up on the good news; unless it was something especially troubling, he didn't want to hear about any problems because it depressed him. When the phone rang today, I picked it up quickly. As hoped, it was Dad.

I tried to figure out a way to tell him what was happening, but he interrupted before I got a chance.

"Suelyn, what's going on? Your mother told me last week that all the money is gone. There was a lot of money. How could it all be gone?"

I don't know what "a lot" meant to my father, but he was upset.

"Well, Dad, you know how bad Mom is with finances when you're not here to handle the bills," I said, trying to buy a little time.

He was no help. He just kept saying there was a lot of money, so our call soon ended.

Now, I was worried about her disease *and* an addiction. She'd been buying drugs for herself and her friends. Maybe that's where all the money went.

At that moment, all I wanted to do was bring all of this to a crashing, dramatic end. I wanted to take away any drugs she had on her—or in her room or in the house, for that matter. If I found it, there would be no way she could deny that she was using them.

I figured it was close by—in her bra, her bag—somewhere close, so I went to her room, with her following close behind all the way. I took her bag and dumped it on the bed. She was furious, close to becoming violent. I'd never seen her like this in my life; she was over the top, almost in a crazed frenzy. She started hitting my arm and trying to grab the bag as I was going through each of its little pockets and zippered compartments.

I found nothing, but she kept hitting and yelling at me. It was horrible, like a scene from a bad movie. Finding nothing, she grabbed her purse and retreated to the corner of the room. "See, you have found *nothing*! I don't have *anything*."

But it didn't end with that; in fact, it got worse.

It dawned on me that she must have it on her, so I started going through her pockets. Even though she flailed at me, I was determined to find it. Finally, I pulled open her blouse, popping off several buttons in the process. Nothing there. To say it was a humiliating moment for both of us would be the proverbial understatement of a lifetime.

She screamed and fought, but I held her back and began pulling her pants down.

I love and respect my mother, I kept thinking. *That's why I'm doing this.* I was trying to stay on course and not give in until I could confront her with the proof, so I kept pulling until a sanitary pad fell out on the floor. It had a rip in the side and when it fell, two cellophane packets of cocaine dropped out.

"Mom, why didn't you tell me about this?" I said, starting to cry. Then she started to cry and we both fell onto the bed.

"You're my best friend. I love you so much," she said, which is exactly what I was going to say.

"You know, all this is difficult for me. Your father's in jail; I've got Lupus. I get so depressed and tired. It seemed to be the only thing that could perk me up and make me forget all that."

We were both exhausted. While my two sisters stood in the hallway crying, I picked up the packets and flushed them down the toilet. I returned to the bedroom, gave Mom a hug, and put her to bed. Then I calmed the girls down and put them to bed. "Tomorrow is going to be a better day. We'll talk then," I told them.

Instead of sleeping in my old room, I climbed into bed with my mother, who was still sobbing. I put my arm around her and nestled under the covers. Before long, we were both sleeping soundly.

The next day when things were quiet, I got out one of my journals . . .

@ ^^ # ^^ *&%* (**@~~@ ##^^^##@9 *)__++

##@^^^%%%6 **^^—) 00 {{{# @@!!.
@ ^^ # ^^ *&%* (**@~~@ ##^^^##@9 *)__++

##@^^^%%%6 **^^—) 00 {{{# @@!!.

Responsibility is a bitch, a burden. It's so hard being me, being 21 and having all these responsibilities. I find it difficult to breathe, I began.

All I want to do is leave Peter's and not depend on him. The longer I live here in his mansion, the more I owe him. Yes, everything is free and I don't have to do anything, but I fear the day will soon come when that will change.

Peter has done so much for my family, and I owe him for that. But I also must be able to provide for them, which is becoming increasingly more expensive to do. When my phone rings and I see that it's my mother calling, my stomach flips because I know she is going to need something else. What will it be this time? What is the problem now?

It's never, "How are you doing, baby? Is everything okay?" I know she sees me as the rock, the pillar—a role in which I've put myself—but sometimes it just gets to be too much. Then, I feel guilty for being angry for wanting her to do something for herself once in a while, to solve her own problems. I feel even guiltier for getting angry at her for doing drugs and frittering away so much of the money I gave her. Why am I the one feeling guilty?

It's a vicious cycle, just one guilty feeling after another. If I buy a blouse, I feel guilty for not saving it to give to my family. While my friends are worrying about whether they will have the money to pay for a dress for the party this weekend, I'm worrying about whether I'll have enough to pay my family's rent and buy them groceries.

I'm rambling now and I know it. @ ^^ # ^^ *&%* (**@~~~@ ##^^^##@9 *)__++

##@^^^%%%6 **^^—) 00 {{{# @@!!.

How about the utility bills? I'm sitting here in the lap of luxury, not having to worry about anything and yet, I'm worrying more about life than my mother, who has nothing. I'm getting it from both sides: my guilt about Peter and my guilt about my mother, but I'm also that other little person on my left shoulder that's saying, "Suelyn, you asked for this, so you've got it."

My mother's Lupus treatments and medications are always looming as well. My sisters need her; I can't raise them on my own, can I? Yes, I'm booking a lot of work, but how long will that last? I'm essentially a freelancer, another choice I've made on my own—running my own business and my own life is the only way, but there are no guarantees. I don't really have a job. I only have what I can make out of my own life.

I feel the weight of the world on my shoulders. My father is helpless behind bars and can't help. Meanwhile my mother is helpless. I am the hope of the family. The men in my life have all set traps for me like hunters in a blind—waiting, waiting, waiting for the unknowing deer to step in the clamp.

I must be strong, I tell myself in my cryptic writings. I must be wise. I must be one-step ahead of everyone else. I must use my brains, my instincts, my talents, and fight to succeed. I *will* succeed. After all, I'm all I have.

End of journal entry.

I LOOK BACK NOW AT that entry, at so many of them, and I see a young woman struggling to find peace and a million answers. I think that's why God gives the young so much energy and drive. Without it, we'd dissolve into a puddle of goo and wallow in our own self-pity.

I like reading these entries because I can see the building blocks that I piled, one on another, to get above and beyond all the pain, guilt, and indecision. How can you not make mistakes when you're not yet even wise enough to make decisions? I revel in the growing process, then feel great angst about all the searching that I know everyone else goes through as well—except for the lazy, the outlaws, the ones who have no conscious or compassion while I, on the other hand, would rather go through the painful learning process.

As for my mother and her challenges, I can only say that I love her dearly. I know that, like all of us, she is just human. No one goes through this life unscathed. We all deal with everything the best we can. No matter how disappointed I might have been about my mother's drug use, I know she, too, must have been just as disappointed with me on numerous occasions. None of us is perfect, which is merely one of the things that makes us all so interesting.

I love all my people, my immediate family and my extended family. We are all good people just trying to do the best we can. I try not to judge anyone anymore. The only person in life I can control is *me*, which is a tough enough job in and of itself!

B RIGHT AND EARLY THE next morning, my mother woke up in a great mood, as if nothing had happened, and made us breakfast. She had the table set nicely and as she served us, she waltzed around singing hymns and just glowing.

"We should all go out together and do something fun. It's so nice out," she sang.

I agreed, anything to keep the mood going. I got the car, piled everyone in and we went shopping, mostly window-shopping and just trying things on. We had ice cream together and then later, a nice lunch—what I would call a normal, fun day for the family.

The weather was so beautiful, when we returned, I left my mother in the apartment and took my sisters to the park so that I could have a heart-to-heart talk with them. I chose a quiet spot under a large tree near the pond where we sat on the grass.

"Girls, you know how much I love you both," is how I started. "I know you are going through some very rough times that you shouldn't have to deal with; I'm sorry you had to see all that last night.

"I just want you to know that this is going to end. Things are going to get better. I just wish you would've told me earlier. I could have spared you," I paused.

"Sue, we know how much you do for us already," Evelyn said, "and how much you already have to deal with; we didn't want to put more pressure on you."

"Listen, I'm going to take care of this. I'm going to find Mom the best rehab center I can. We are going to get her help. She's going to get better. I don't want you girls to worry about this," I told them. Both were listening intently.

"I am going to find you all a good place to live near me in California—get you out of Queens and close to me. You're going to go to the best school, make great friends, and be happy," I said, knowing if I could have them close, I could keep an eye on my mother. "You girls have a beautiful future. You're smart and beautiful, and I'm going to make sure everything is okay."

My speech seemed to put them at ease, at least temporarily. This was my solution, my only solution. I didn't want my mother in a rehab center in Queens. I wanted the therapy to "take," which meant being there when she got out. I knew it didn't end with just a week or a month in a facility.

I began to plan immediately. After we returned to the house to find that our mother was still singing, the girls went to their rooms while I started making calls and formulating a plan.

I had told the girls to pack only the important things. We weren't going to bring any furniture. I would have to arrange for a van large enough to bring the Jeep Cherokee so my mother would have transportation, but little else. We packed clothes, the flat screen TV, my father's expensive tools, and that was about it. My mother put up no argument and even felt California was a great idea. I don't like loose ends, so everything was settled quickly. However, in orchestrating the move, and not being in California, I still had to find them an apartment; so, for the time being, I put them up in my room at Peter's house.

As soon as we settled in, I went apartment hunting and found them a nice place in the Valley in Sherman Oaks, about 30 minutes away. Peter wasn't home much, but that weekend he was, which couldn't have been worse timing. He'd come in for the weekend to have some parties, and I didn't want my sisters around all that drinking and, honestly, I didn't want him around them. I just didn't want them to see that world. Then I started thinking; I had to get them out of New York, get my mother away from her "friends," but now I've brought them to southern California, party central. But I didn't have a choice. After all, we never get everything we want.

The apartment I found was only a one-bedroom but it was cute and available as a month-to-month rental. I wanted to get them settled quickly and then later, find something larger and, hopefully, closer to Marina Del Rey.

For the next couple of weeks, we had fun decorating the apartment, painting, buying furniture, getting them settled, and finding the girls a school. The last order of business was to find my mother a rehab facility, which, as you can imagine, went over like a lead balloon.

Mom fought me—loudly. I always made sure the discussions took place when the girls were out. She tried every trick in the book, saying, "You're not the mother of me. *I* am the mother. You're just throwing me out now that I'm old." My mother can be very dramatic, but I anticipated all of her arguments.

"You're only 47. You're not old, Mom. I'm not throwing you out. I'm trying to help you." I used every argument I could muster. I didn't know that much about drug recovery, but I'd seen more than my share of drugs and I hated them. I didn't want her to get into them any deeper. I had to nip this in the bud and if she wouldn't go into a temporary facility, I knew I would have to put her up in a permanent one.

Except for my common sense and love for my family, which was enough, I otherwise had no help or guidance. It was difficult talking with my father from prison. You can't say much when someone is listening in, so all I told him was that I had brought the girls and Mom to California to give them a better life.

I knew the apartment was small, but depending upon when my father got out, I'd either move them closer to me later or, when he was released, they would probably all go back to Brazil because we knew he would undoubtedly be deported then.

I got the girls enrolled in school. Their apartment complex was safe, in a good neighborhood, and included plenty of amenities. The next order of business was to get my mother treatment. I enrolled her in a rehab center in Sherman Oaks where she attended meetings much like those conducted at AA. That way, she could continue to take care of the girls and, hopefully, stay away from drugs on an outpatient basis. She had no friends in the Valley, therefore no contacts or bad influences. I hoped that this more controlled environment would do the trick. It certainly was far better for the girls. At the same time, I lined her up with a medical facility where she could get her treatments for Lupus.

At this point, all was going as well as I could expect. But then Peter's mother, who was old, became very ill, was hospitalized, and then died. Although she'd had a heart transplant, in the end it failed, so Peter became very interested in stem cell research and the possibilities of stem cells as a cure for many things. He was distraught and wanted to explore his own options.

The women in his life I'd gotten to know—his mother, sister, ex-wife, and daughters—were all weak and fragile. His mother had just died at the age of 98 and after that, he really changed and became more sensitive. He also became obsessed with preventative medicine and anti-aging treatments. He'd always been an avid sportsman and looked great for his age, but he was closing in on 70, and, because he didn't like the idea of slowing down or getting sick, he wanted to enjoy his life forever, or at least into his hundreds.

During the last year I lived with Peter in Marina Del Rey, he was involved with stem cell treatments and exercising daily. One day, during a trip to Kiev, Ukraine, where he was having stem cell research done (the same thing my Mother was going to do for her Lupus in a few weeks), when he was finished, he said he had to talk to me about something. He took me into a board meeting-type room with a large table surrounded by about 30 chairs. After we sat down, he asked, "Suelyn, do you know what the best stem cells are?"

Having done a lot of research for my mother, I said, "Yes, embryonic."

"Correct! And you know what? If you got pregnant and had an abortion, we could use those embryonic cells and have a life supply for all of us: you, your mother, and me. A lot of people are doing it," he said enthusiastically.

I was beyond stunned. This was the sickest thing I'd ever heard Peter say. I thought he was going crazy. But looking back now, I realize that his obsession had taken him to a dark and very off-kilter place in his mind.

I couldn't speak for a moment. Finally, catching my breath, I said, "Peter, I do *not* believe in abortion."

"Suelyn, this is the way to save your mother and to keep me alive so I can take care of all of us," he said passionately.

I just shook my head no, but he kept talking.

"Suelyn, I would compensate you extremely well. We could set up your mother's treatment and do it all during the same trip," he said with a wink.

Ultimately acquiescing, we later found a better place for my mother—a treatment facility in Shanghai, China—where she was eventually treated. Peter paid all the expenses, including the $60,000 treatment costs. The week before my mother's treatment, my father was deported to Brazil again where my mother and sisters would be moving to be close to him.

The trip to China was a very hectic time. Peter was amazing, but I also knew what was coming, what it would cost me.

I spent my nights wrestling with whether I should do what he had asked, night after night after night, until I was consumed with angst and guilt.

At first, I'd only been worried about our relationship: Could I keep it platonic; could I continue to be his arm candy? But now, there was much more at stake—my soul. Of course, my parents saw only Peter's kindness and generosity. They knew nothing of what I was going through, the price I might have to pay. I began to have nightmares about Peter. In the dreams, he was the devil, but he was dressed in an Armani suit and looked normal. He kept giving me everything, things I didn't ask for, but things like my mother's treatment and help in Brazil—all meant to be enticing—but, of course, there was always the price I had to pay. I thought that if I gathered up all my savings, it might be enough for me to pay for a house outright for my family, furnish it, and make sure they were taken care of, while still having enough left over for me to survive. My thoughts began to drift to this solution. I knew I would have to invest in something to make my money grow. If it took a few years, I would be able to pull it all off without any help.

Having just settled in California, my sisters were not happy about moving to Brazil. However, we looked at apartments there and, stalling for more time, I kept turning them all down. This one wasn't big enough, that one didn't have enough windows, this one was on the wrong side of town, etc. Meanwhile, my parents and sisters were staying with my grandmother and after I returned to the U.S., I sent them enough money to choose whatever apartment they wanted, along with a car so they could get around and my father to work once he settled in and started looking for a job.

When I told Peter about everything, he offered to put everyone, including him and me, along with all of my family's belongings, on his private plane, to fly us down to Rio. My mother's treatments were over and we'd returned from China, but I'm not sure how much any of it accomplished.

This was in April, right after Carnival, and I thought his offer was not only wonderful, but very generous as well. I knew it was going to be difficult on them. At the age of 50, it would be difficult for my father to get steady work, I was also aware that jail had taken a lot out of him so I worried all the time about them. Nonetheless, after they found an apartment and everything was moved in, Peter and I returned to California.

When the dust settled a little and we were back in Marina Del Rey, Peter became obsessed, not only with living forever, but about looking younger. For the time being, the abortion idea had been shelved. One day he even joked with my mother and sisters, saying, "I'm working out hard so I can get my muscles big and have a six-pack like the guys Suelyn likes. "Maybe then, she'll fall in love with me."

I thought, *This is the silliest thing I've ever heard!*

Peter and I were in Abu Dabi, and I was just getting ready to shoot my reality show. After a long day of meetings and deals, we were having a relaxing dinner with a large group of people at the Khalifa, one of the tallest buildings in the world.

When Peter and I walked outside to a massive balcony with a view of the city that was breathtaking, he said, "You know what I was thinking?"

Here we go again.

"What?"

"Once your show kicks off, we should start planning something big."

"What do you mean?"

"What with all the bad press on the DUI and all, we should do something a little different," he said cryptically.

"Like what?"

"We should have a big wedding, the best one the world has ever seen," he answered, smiling and completely serious.

"What?" I said with an expression to match.

To clarify, he said, "Oh, it would be a prank wedding, a joke. We could do the whole set up and then at the last second, tell everyone it was just a big joke."

I shook my head. "Come on, Peter. Let's go inside. It's been a long day."

I invested a year in starting up my career. I traveled with Peter as well as alone to different factories all over the world, looking for fabrics, selecting the perfect blends, patterns, and textures so that everything would be perfect. Although Peter had invested in me, I'd also put a lot of my own money into the enterprise in addition to sending my family money every month.

Although I was making a great deal of money, I was also spending a great deal of money. I started going to numerous events, meeting extravagant people and getting extravagant offers, one of which was a booking in Dubai. A prince wanted me to come to his birthday party and just hang out. He paid me $50,000 for about three hours of "hanging out."

After that came the offers for "club hosting," which is lucrative, particularly in comparison to the actual work performed. For example, suppose it's going to be Labor Day weekend soon and a club wants to create a buzz for the holiday, or is celebrating its anniversary, or just wants to drum up business: they promote a celebrity, model, actress, or singer for the event. They will advertise with flyers or through the media that a particular celebrity is going to be there. If I'm the one they're promoting, they pay me a fee to be the "host," which means I'm expected to show up, sit at my own VIP table, sign autographs, and talk to the people who are at the club—otherwise known as "chatting it up." They provide the drinks, of course; and they encourage me to bring a few friends as well.

I was also expected to have my picture taken with fans and stick around for at least a couple of hours. What could be easier than that? I would put on a special dress, have my makeup done, grab some friends, and go to a club until about midnight, for which—depending on the club, the event, and the weekend—I was paid anywhere from $10,000 to $50,000 per appearance.

I was paid even more for hosting clubs out of the country. They even have them for celebrity (and I use that term loosely) birthdays. One year, I did 13 birthday parties, each at a different club, and each telling their customers that this was their "official" birthday party.

I was making exorbitant amounts of money for appearances, modeling, videos, and selling my clothes—yet, I didn't have the power to erase the problems that were so important to me.

I felt so betrayed when I found out my mother had made new connections in Brazil and was using some of the money I sent them each month to buy drugs again. I needed balance now more than at any other time in my life. I was rapidly learning that success isn't all it's cracked up to be. The more money and notoriety you gain, the more problems you have. You cannot necessarily control everything, including your own family. The only thing you can truly control is yourself, your thinking, and your own behavior. If you can do that, and do the right thing at every turn, then you have really accomplished nirvana.

I was traveling all over the world, being exposed to beauty, knowledge, and experiences I could never get living in Queens or Brazil. I was meeting phenomenal people and receiving offers for television shows; filming the Grand Prix and interviewing the drivers on air; and going to the Italian Film Festival. Men were throwing extravagant gifts at me: gold, diamonds, all kinds of jewelry, expensive clothing and, yet, I was very unhappy because the important things in life were missing.

It's funny now, in a way, but with all that going on, oftentimes, all I wanted to do was sit with a man I loved, snuggle, munch on popcorn, and watch an old movie on TV in front of the fireplace. Now *that* sounded like nirvana to me.

<hr>

Meeting Joe

WHOEVER CAME UP WITH the quote, "You never get a second chance to make a first impression," was wrong!

Joe, the man who is now the love of my life, almost didn't make it past the "Suelyn Man Test." Admit it, girls—we all have our barometers and litmus tests. As sure as the measuring stick in front of the roller coaster ride at the fair, "You must be *this* tall to go on *this* ride."

Our ride almost didn't begin, not because Joe was too short, but because he was too obnoxious and full of himself. It was at a party in France. (Hey, if you can't namedrop cities, what's the point of collecting all the passport stamps, right?) I will admit, he did get my attention, but for all the wrong reasons. Yes, he was very handsome, but he did a good job of hiding it under his arrogance. He was drunk and from what I observed (Joe, you know I love you dearly), he was acting very inappropriate.

He carried himself intentionally in a "too cool for school" manner, which I could tell by the way he was parading around and flirting with every girl in the room. His outfit looked like one from those Italian mobster movies. It was like being set back in time, standing right in front of Robert De Niro in a scene of the movie "Casino" to be exact. SMH!!!

Being in the fashion industry and having designed clothes, I was perhaps more judgmental than most, but it's something about which I'm always aware. Clothes say a lot about a man, particularly if he's supposed to be dressing to the nines for a big party.

Anyhow, at that point in my life, I wasn't interested in meeting a man on a personal level anyway, so when we were introduced, all my observations from afar were confirmed. *Is this guy for real?*

Equation: First impression = negative two.

As time went on, more than four or five of my close friends kept bringing him up, telling me how perfect he would be for me. I couldn't understand what these so-called confidants saw in him that I didn't. Since they thought he was perfect, I decided I was really missing something. After all, they couldn't *all* be wrong. Nevertheless, I wasn't interested.

Months later, I bumped into him again, totally by accident (or maybe it was serendipity). It was at a party after the Oscars in L.A. This time, he wasn't dressed like an Italian mobster. He looked like he had just fallen out of a GQ magazine. His thick, copper hair was slicked back very Italianesque. He seemed slimmer, in way better shape. He wore a stunning, $5,000-tailored, black silk suit. He looked like he walked right off a Tom Ford runway show. Visualize it: here's a man six feet + tall, lightly and leanly muscled like a big tiger, The showstopper, however, were his Chrsitian Louboutin (who happens to be my favorite shoe designer) shoes, the ones with the red bottoms. He was sober; clever, even at a distance; and he moved with the grace of a dancer.

What a difference a second impression can make!

I couldn't believe it was the same man. I couldn't have dressed him any better myself, not that I wouldn't have liked to try! So, of course, I checked him out ever so surreptitiously because I didn't, of course, want him to notice that I was noticing him.

Because I had to leave the party early that evening for another engagement, we didn't connect. However, his image remained firmly implanted in the front of my brain (as well as numerous other places!).

The next day, a friend who was there called and said, "Suelyn, Joe is still in town. He's here with me right now. Here he is," she said, handing the phone to him before I could object.

"I saw you at the Oscar party," he began. "I came over to say hello, but you had disappeared like a ghost."

"Oh, I didn't know you were there. I had another party to go to," I said coyly.

He didn't waste a second. "I'd love to take you to dinner."

"Thanks for the invitation; that would be nice, but I'm leaving for the south of France tomorrow." (I always like to add the "south" to the France part. Makes it sound even sexier.)

"Well, how about tonight then?" he asked, not missing a beat.

"I don't know if that will work," I stalled.

"Have you ever been to El Cielo? It's the best Italian restaurant in L.A.," was his quick response, as though he hadn't heard what I'd just said.

"No. Actually, I haven't."

"Come to think of it, do you have plans today, right now? I have a little adventure in mind."

Hmm, what kind of adventure could this hot-blooded Italian have in mind?

"What is it?" I asked, curiosity getting the best of me.

"Let me surprise you. I'll pick you up at two. Where will you be?"

I'd caved in, in only a matter of 15 seconds. His voice dripped through the phone into my ear and down my neck.

"I'll text you the address."

"I don't do texts, but I have a pen and pad of paper."

Huh? Who doesn't text in L.A. in 2011? It's my primary mode of communication. I don't know about you, but I text hundreds of times a day. In fact, I nearly wrote this book texting stories to myself. Frankly, I don't think there are three people on the planet who are faster than I am.

The limo rolled up the broad circular drive. Before I left my room, I knew what he'd be wearing. Though I had an inkling we would be going to dinner at a very nice restaurant, much like the late Steve Jobs, he'd be in what I called the "Joe uniform": jeans, a tight black T-shirt, and a black leather jacket—the jacket as supple as cashmere.

I laughed to myself as I envisioned his closet—a sea of jeans and black, all the same brands. It must look like that of a Catholic priest. *What will I wear today, black, black, or black?* However, he didn't waste time worrying about his wardrobe, there were more important things on his mind, and tonight, that was me.

Though I'd been ready for an hour, I waited just inside the front door. I wanted the chauffeur to ring my doorbell and escort me to the car, but instead, it was Joe who greeted me when I opened the front door. This time he wasn't wearing his sunglasses. I looked into his eyes through my shades. I was immediately mesmerized by his green camouflage eyes. If I stared into his eyes any longer he could have easily hypnotized me.

True to form in his uniform, he kissed my hand, then my lips, and then gave me a gorgeous orchid, the smell filling the atrium.

It was only five p.m. and the weather was like the proverbial southern California postcard. He couldn't have chosen a better day to whisk me away in a helicopter to view the coastal cliffs and Malibu.

After about a 20-minute drive, we parked at a heli-pad next to a sleek black, four-seat helicopter, its giant blades turning like the slowest speed on a ceiling fan.

We climbed in, I put on a helmet with a microphone near my mouth, and off we climbed, quickly soaring over the Pacific, along the beaches of Malibu. I'd been in helicopters before but to do so this time in southern California was special.

As Joe told me about the sights and the various celebrity homes dotting the edge of the beach, I just stared at him. I could have finished each of his sentences, that's how close I felt already; but I kept silent and let him be the guide.

"Next stop, El Cielo," he said.

I'd heard of the restaurant, one of the best in L.A., and I'd been to most of the great ones, but this was a first and turned out to be my favorite, Italian, just like Joe.

We sat in the back in an intimate booth. Before the waiter had even spoken with us, he was magically there with a bottle of cabernet. Joe gently lifted the cork to his nose, nodding that it was to his liking, and then he made a toast.

I'm not a wine connoisseur by any means, but this silky red was so full of flavor and spice, I didn't want it to trickle down my throat, preferring instead to let it nestle on the back of my tongue.

There were three distinctive candles on the impeccable starched white linen tablecloth, each offering a different scent. Curious and wanting to smell one, I reached across my place setting and picked one up. However, when I pulled it back toward me, a glob of hot wax spewed out, falling directly into my cleavage, which was fully exposed by my black cocktail dress.

"Yow!" I screamed. Although it was scalding, it quickly cooled to a grayish white lump. I didn't touch it, but we were both looking at it when he asked, "Are you alright?"

"Yes," I responded, still staring at the wax. He looked at the lump and then I looked again, then we both looked at each other, knowing exactly what it looked like. Neither of us said a word before we both cracked up.

As we sipped our wine, we talked about how much we had in common, which was almost spooky. We shared the same family values and beliefs—our loved ones always came first. We both had strong personalities and were natural born fighters who quickly spoke our minds, without hesitation. We were both the firstborns, and we couldn't stand things left unfinished—the list went on and on. It was obvious that we fit like the proverbial hand and glove.

After we ordered, I excused myself and went to the restroom to check my make-up. Staring into the mirror, I asked and answered my own question—is he *the one?* But then, my thoughts drifted off into another direction.

It seems in life that nothing is ever perfect. There must always be a balance. I didn't really learn that lesson until later that year when

I realized that is all part of the universal plan, part of the growing and learning. My problem was that I was still living at Peter's place in Marina del Rey, only that was just one part of the movie. With his mentoring, I was also launching my clothing line and was deeply involved in all the resources to which he introduced me. As a result of his worldwide reputation, clout, and respect, I was able to contract with factories in India and China to make some of my creations, his company was providing the shipping—the list went on and on. However, the third unfortunate point on this triangle was that Peter was obsessed with me and my success.

At the age of 25, I was working hard. I was also getting parts in major movies and was about to start filming a reality show that summer, which was set to shoot at Peter's house. The word "Bombshell" for my clothes was my idea, and I'd invested a lot of my own money in the line.

Peter was my official cheerleader. Knowing how strong my work ethic was, he tutored me well. He saw a great deal of creative potential as well and wanted to help me reach the next level, and then the next, and then the next. He understood the fashion world like nobody else. He was an enormous, larger-than-life empire builder, and he wanted us to stay connected. He would always joke, "When you get big, don't forget the little people," and then he'd point at himself and smile. But behind that smile and those twinkling eyes was a very calculating, smart, and aggressive man who peed on every bush that surrounded his kingdom, sometimes three times a day.

Of course, I had put in my time and a huge amount of effort on my own behalf toward the development of my clothing line as well as understanding his world of business. I attended so many meetings with him, I lost track. With his permission, of course, I listened to hundreds of his business calls, and I sat late into the evenings with him near his fireplace, listening to his endless business stories. I was the lucky recipient of a first-class education. I had a front row seat, not at a stuffy university filled with books and lectures, but right in the thick of it, beside a true mover and shaker who never missed dotting an *i* or crossing a *t*.

Peter was the consummate entrepreneur, and I was the voracious student. Now, how could I tell him about Joe? How could I tell him I'd be moving to my own place?

Peter was a top-notch teacher. We had a deal between us; it wasn't even verbal, it was just understood. I was his protégé. I lived in his mansion, free of charge. I also had a staff working for my every need, a cook, maids, and an assistant. Additionally, I had access to the cars and a company American Express card that started with a $5,000 monthly limit.

Peter always complimented me on my style and, with time, after discovering that I had my own eye for fashion, I gave Peter great ideas for his many lines of clothes. My day-to-day life revolved around working with all the details of my clothing line but when Peter called and said he needed me at an important event or meeting, I would drop everything and go. It made him feel good to have me on his arm, at his side, which I accommodated because of all he had done and was still doing for me, including depositing bonuses into my account. Let's face it: I was a kept woman who tried to keep her distance and did, but only sexually because that just wasn't in the cards.

With time, even as grateful as I was for all that he was doing, I began to resent the "arm candy" thing, something I never wanted to be, but had found myself pulled into, albeit ever so gently. I was the oblivious frog that was being boiled—again, albeit ever so gently.

Eventually, Peter wanted to go to more and more events, all the big ones to, of course, show me off. It didn't feel right, and it was getting more and more wrong every day. I was falling into the "obligation" thing, the guilt thing. I was torn. He'd helped me so much. I never would have been able to accomplish the things I had at the age of 25 without his help and mentoring, and, yet, at times I was nothing more than an attractive piece of flesh, no more, no less.

He had many women at his beck and call anytime, but I was his number one choice, at least according to him. After a while, I was getting to the point where I didn't want to be seen with him.

One night at a big party, when I was feeling particularly used, as he held me around my waist, he told a circle of friends, "Suelyn is the smartest woman I've ever known for her age. She speaks so many languages, loves to win every game she plays and fears nothing."

His other girls hated all this, of course.

I, in turn, complimented him all the time, elevating his ego. Although I don't think he really needed it, he did like hearing it from me. When I said something nice about him in front of others, his blue eyes would sparkle with joy and his smile would stretch from ear to ear.

I was learning everything about Peter's emotions, traits, and habits and as I have always been able to do with everyone else around me, became very good at reading him. I knew when he was angry, upset, sad, or happy without him saying a single word, which is one of the reasons he trusted me. He shared his fears and his dreams with me and wanted me to do the same.

Peter often professed his love for me in his own way, but I always made it clear that I wasn't looking at him in "that way." Being "friends" and "lovers" are mutually exclusive emotions, which is oftentimes a shame because your lover should also be your best friend. Unfortunately, it just didn't work that way for me, especially because of the setting in which I found myself.

Not that Peter didn't try to make me fall for him, but I showed no interest in a love relationship at all.

The point is, he got a kick out of how fast I learned things, how competitive and driven I was, and he loved testing it all for his own amusement. He always said how great it would be if one of his kids had been like me.

It was fate, even if it took a little while. We could not be more perfect for each other. If I'd met Joe earlier in my life, it never would have worked. We have both been through a lot in our lives and traveled extensively. In fact, when we compared our passports over wine one evening, we found that we'd been in the same countries at the same time, on different planes, but at the exact same times.

Sometimes, I think the love Gods have plans to which we aren't privy. It just goes to show you that you have to be open. You can't judge books by their covers; you must, at the very least, read a few pages.

We are so dynamic together with so much electricity going on that I often notice people staring at us (no, this isn't ego). People go out of their way to stare and judging by their expressions, they often seem bothered by us, even though they don't know us. We've even had some problems with aggressive strangers. I'm not sure why, but I've always felt safe because Joe is very confident, while also very humble and peaceful. He's a licensed professional boxer who always wears a big smile on his face.

I love my Joe dearly. I know I am blessed to have him in my life. I know I'm a handful and that I'm very independent, but with Joe I feel protected and able to be myself completely, at all times, which shows me how confident he is with himself and his love for me.

Although Joe is 11 years older than I am, we are evenly matched in every way. I personally think men need a little more time to catch up with women, but that's alright—when you meet the right one, it's worth the wait.

Love you, baby!

A Love Letter to Joe

J OE HAS ALWAYS BEEN a gentleman, which I soon learned came directly from his parents' DNA. When he suspected I was ready, he *proposed* that I become his girlfriend. For a moment, I thought he was going to get down on one knee.

A week after I said yes, he insisted I go with him to Canada to meet his family. His parents were the most grounded human beings I'd ever met and an inspiration for common sense and loving relationships.

During dinner the first night in their beautiful Toronto home, I saw a bond I never knew was possible. You wouldn't call their home a house; it was a true *home* complete with the smell of lavender, a sense of serenity, and a certain underlying energy. I was at peace there.

As I'd gotten to know Joe, I also realized that this was the only place he could have been raised by two extraordinary parents that taught him the virtues of good manners and ethics, and gave him a strong moral compass to follow. Although I already knew he was the genuine thing, his parents and their home just solidified that knowledge.

His mother was as sweet as honey and soft as warm butter. His father was strong and wise. What a blend—a combination that made Joe a gentleman who could be the sweetest man in the world but still kill to protect what he loved. I'm not only in love with him: I also like him a lot as a person and a man.

I love to watch him and listen to him when he talks. Sometimes he stutters when he's really nervous. I love how intense he is when he's in the ring boxing, one of his passions. I love how he eats, sleeps, and walks (can you tell I'm in love?), and I love that he loves me.

I am safe, happy, and secure.

The walls I'd always put up against everyone else (which turned out to be great instincts, by the way) weren't placed there for him. I could feel his blend of strength and compassion.

I often ask myself, *How is it possible to love someone and then love them even more for their faults?* After knowing him for only a couple of hours, my first thought was, *Wow, he is just like me. We're a perfect fit!* But, of course, that thought quickly dissolved when I realized that opposites do attract. I'm the futurist; he's the caveman. While that may be difficult for some to understand, the combination makes perfect sense to me.

Joe writes everything down slowly and deliberately by hand. He'll call someone 50 times in a relentless effort to resolve anything that is important to him, and most everything is. He hates electronics and computers, preferring to process everything in his brain. He is actually clueless about the Internet or how to use it, which is, of course, the complete antitheses of me who has been known to write five pages of small copy on my Blackberry several times a day.

He doesn't even know what Twitter, Facebook, My Space, and all the others are or what they do. Somehow, though, our different worlds and ways cross paths all day long, and they work. He's always trying to slow me down, and I'm always trying to speed him up and in between those two, we meet and share the best moments possible.

Even though they were already aware, I shared all of these things with his parents, knowing they already understood.

Then it was time to visit my parents. After we returned to L.A. from Canada, I set it up. My parents didn't have any room in their tiny place so we stayed at a nearby hotel.

Even though I was very nervous, we were going to Brazil. My father had only recently been released from prison. They were all just getting their sea legs again and starting from scratch. *How could I possibly explain everything to Joe?* Not only did he have to adjust to the country, but the culture as well—the culture of my family.

On the flight down, I worried. *Am I doing the right thing? Have I acted too quickly, merely in response to his father and mother? Is it too soon to share with my family after having just shared it all with Joe's parents?*

Even though we were already on the plane, my final decision was to drop all the walls—the barriers—and have no lies, nothing to hide—just be me and let my parents be themselves. Take it or leave it.

Joe asked me to be his girlfriend on our second date. He was perfect for me, everything I wanted.

Knowing that he wasn't comfortable that I was living in Peter's house, I agreed to move out. It was at the time that I was trying to move out of Peter's and find my own place anyhow. Besides, I knew I had to get out before it was too late.

Joe was aware of part of my "situation," but he didn't know all the details. He was from Toronto, which oddly was where Peter called home, too, because that's where he'd built his fashion empire.

Within the week, Joe and I were looking for a place to share and finally found one on a major street in Los Angeles. It went so smoothly that within days, we were living together, all cozy and happy, and I was finally out of Peter's forever. While I was free at last, I was nervous about what would happen to my clothing line without all of his connections.

We had pulled up days before in front of Peter's mansion, and Joe helped me pack all my stuff, carefully arranging it in the moving truck. I don't know how he managed to squeeze it all in without breaking a single thing, but he did.

Since Peter was still in Toronto, I knew I had to move out before he got back. Joe and I stayed at the Ritz-Carlton for the next week until our new place was ready. When it was and I first stepped off the elevator into "our" living room, I took a deep breath, exhaled with a giant sigh, and said, "I did it!"

Once we'd moved in, my first priority was to organize my closet. Then I wanted to get unique custom furniture. Everything needed to be castle-esque—large, a bit ostentatious, luxurious, befitting for a queen and king.

As if the designer had been reading my mind when he designed them, I found the most amazing chairs—black velour, tall, with sparkling buttons all over them. They were right out of a fairy tale resembling thrones for royalty. Since we had the space for oversized furniture, I was determined to use it!

I love candles, so I went crazy with them. We had two large black candles made; they weighed 80 pounds each and were as big as a six-year-old child.

It took a while, but the decorating was finally complete (not everything was black, by the way) and it was time to show it off at a house-warming party. All we needed was a dining room table and chairs for our castle high above Wilshire. I found the perfect table, again fit for royalty that would seat 12. The centerpiece consisted of a massive assortment of all the candles I had selected.

I spent two weeks handling the invitations. I hired two dancers with theme outfits and chose a DJ, photographers, and videographers. We had four bartenders, a sushi cook, and a near-naked sushi girl, lying across the dining room table (which, of course, we cleaned well before serving dinner). The party was a huge success, and everyone had a blast.

Then, two weeks later, the worst possible thing happened. When I woke up one morning and looked at my phone on the bed stand, it showed 80 missed calls. Déjà vu back to my night of the DUI! I reached over and quickly listened to the first message from a girlfriend. "Suelyn, you have a sex tape out. It's all over the Internet."

Oh my God! How could this be happening? I had never been in any sex tapes, or even any sexual photos aside from lingerie—nothing. What was going on?

The next message was from my mother. I returned the call immediately. When she picked up the phone, she was crying.

"Baby, what's going on?" she sobbed. "How did you and Joe let this happen?"

"What are you talking about, Mom?"

"Suelyn, everyone is messaging your sisters on Facebook, and I just saw on the Internet how you and Joe released a sex tape. It shows everything, Suelyn, and I mean *everything!*

I shook my head, trying to come out of my nightmare but was quickly learning that it wasn't a dream.

"Don't worry, Mom. It's a fake. I'm going to take care of it. I've never done any sex tapes!" I said angrily.

"Suelyn, this is *not* a fake. This is you and Joe. I saw it with my own eyes. Oh my God!" she said in that Catholic voice of hers.

"I'll call you back, Mom."

As I was beginning to perspire and shake, Joe entered the room. He'd just come back from the gym and stopped when he saw the expression—the horror—on my face.

"What's the matter, baby?" he asked, coming over and sitting on the edge of the bed next to me.

"You're not going to believe it, Joe. There's a sex tape of us out on the Internet."

"What? How? That's impossible. Who filmed us? We've never done anything like that," and then we had an "aha" moment. I could see it on his face at the same time I could feel it on mine. We ran into the office and started the computer and there it was, the montage of photos and videos we'd done in our bedroom a month before, the one I had on my laptop. In all the frivolity and noise, someone had slipped a thumb drive into the computer and downloaded a copy.

In the ensuing weeks, they'd had time to edit and tamper with it before releasing it.

I was beyond humiliated. We were in a haze as we continued to stare at the horror before us. As the anger over the theft ultimately turned to regret, we began to run through all of the "what-ifs" that accompany guilt. Joe was thinking about his business, his business partners, his family, his reputation.

As for me, I paced the office in circles, thinking that it was about the worst thing in the world that could happen. My career was over, plus everyone in my family had already seen it all. This was not how I wanted to be viewed by the world. Now, I had a DUI and a sex tape all over the Internet, and no one to blame but myself. I could only imagine what my family and friends were thinking, what Joe's people were thinking. It was bleak, disgraceful, and shameful. I have never felt so exposed and unprotected as I felt at that moment.

The first person I called was my agent. Before I even had a chance to talk, he said, "Hey, Suelyn, great video! This'll get great press coverage."

"Are you kidding me? Are you drinking this early?" I screamed. "I didn't put that out. Someone stole my laptop the night of our house-warming party. That was a private video Joe and I did for *us*, for *our* eyes only. This is horrible! How could you think I would put something like that out?"

"Oh, I'm sorry. Of course not."

"This is the absolute worst thing that could happen to my career, not to mention my life."

"Well, the first thing we need to do is hire a lawyer and find out who did this and get it taken down."

"You can't get it 'taken down,'" I said, now becoming nearly hysterical.

People talked about the video for months. It became the focal point of my life. I felt like I was going to crack—so did Joe. We had to get away, though I knew that anywhere I went, there *I* was. There was no getting away from the Internet or myself. Nevertheless, we planned a trip to Rome—anything for a change of scenery.

After a few days there—the different tempo, faces, and sights—I began to breathe more easily again. We went to the Vatican (of all places). We went to several great restaurants. We were incognito, wearing large sunglasses and hats, until one morning at a café down the street from our hotel, we noticed that a paparazzi was stalking us. When he snuck up on me, he asked about the sex tape, wanting to know when was I going to do the next one. I wanted to stab him with my fork.

Then, Nickelodeon dropped me from a movie, of course, and everything ultimately reverted to the nightmare in Los Angeles. Like I always say, "Wherever *you* go, there *you* are." Mistakes and bad judgments invariably come back to haunt you.

The Nickelodeon deal really hurt. I'd wanted to do the movie for kids so much. I wanted to try something different, and that was going to be my entree.

Editorial

I N INTERVIEWS, EVEN THOUGH I'm still young, I'm often asked for my advice for young girls because of what I've been through, being a woman in a man's world, making my own way in business and, of course, some of the media stories.

I have a passion to help young girls for all these reasons. I hate when I hear that some young girls think it's funny when some celebrity acts like an idiot, gets drunk, does drugs, or pulls a Charlie Sheen act, so not winning. I hate it when they are confused and look up to the wrong people, who are just images reflected outwardly for the public.

I want girls to understand that fame and fortune are rarely what they appear to be. It's so easy to be dragged around by money, material things that are meaningless, or admiring jerks.

I tell all the girls I talk with that if they only do one thing right, "Just be yourself." Of course, that's easier said than done because a lot of them don't know who they are or what they really want, so they create a fantasy world filled with the types of people they see in music, film, or sports. It's a false world, kind of like a Disneyland for adults who should know better.

On the other hand, I encourage them to find mentors, good people from whom they can truly learn. With the exception of only a couple of relationships, I was always lucky to have a lot of drive of my own and then be surrounded by bright, caring people, too. Hey, you've gotta learn from your mistakes, right?

Don't try to be like other people. Invent yourself if you don't know who you are yet. Forget the surgery, the boob jobs, all of it. Every woman has her own unique talents, qualities, and passions. I think the best thing a young girl can do is learn how to make the most of her own strengths.

You don't have to be a concert pianist, if that's not in the cards for you. You don't have to be a movie star, singer, or model, if that's not what you want to do. Becoming satisfied and perhaps even successful at something that is honest and is *you* is far more important, no matter what "it" may be.

It's better to be the first-rated version of yourself than to be the second-rated version of someone else.

Don't try to live other people's lives. Why would you want to borrow someone else's dreams? Think of all the wasted energy you expend trying to duplicate someone else's passion. You can't succeed at it anyway, so why waste all your time—and life—trying to do so?

There's no one quite as strong willed, confident, smart, and beautiful as a young girl who knows who she is and what she wants. Finding it and following that desire builds character, because the truly worthy endeavors take a lot of work.

Now, I'm not advocating lying, but it is sometimes necessary to "fake it until you make it," as I did on my first modeling jobs and getting those first photos taken by my friend.

I believe that's okay if what you're trying to do is in your blood, is what you're good at in your heart, and is what you want more than anything else in the world. The only reason you oftentimes need to "fake it" is because that's sometimes the only way a young girl will be taken seriously in the business world.

When you're just starting, you're caught between the proverbial rock and hard spot. How can you get a job if you don't have experience, and how can you get the experience if no one will hire you?

My entire life, albeit as short as it's been thus far, I have just jumped in with both feet in everything I wanted to do, because I knew I knew it; I knew I'd be good at it if I just had the chance to prove it. I loved whatever I was going after, which was enough for the moment.

I truly believe that if you take a little different perspective on the way our culture and society look at things, you'll find yourself achieving what you want as long as you always do the right thing, which means following the Golden Rule.

In Western society, failure is frowned upon; there isn't any room for mistakes. Mistakes will get you fired, ridiculed, shunned, and/or banished.

In reality, it's the mistakes we make that provide the grease that makes the wheels turn. No entrepreneur, accomplished writer, musician, actor, scientist, artist, chef, model, designer, singer, or racecar driver, to mention but a few, ever *really* make it to the top of their profession without making a lot of mistakes.

We are humans. We have to learn as we grow, and the learning is what makes us grow. In the animal world, a newborn colt is out of the womb, on the grass, and up and running within an hour. It takes us about a year, and then only after a few spills, bumps, and cracked skulls. For example, that's why we have electricity: It took Thomas Edison 99 failures (or mistakes) before he invented a usable light bulb, which means he was wrong 99-percent of the time. Hopefully, you and I won't fail that often.

Young people have to understand they aren't colts or mares; they have to fight for what they want, and they have to make plenty of mistakes. If our society could look at mistakes as the steppingstones, as the markers of those who have the most potential because they are the ones who keep getting up and getting back into the fight, then we would all be a lot better off.

Be yourself. If you don't know who that is, find a mentor, experiment, dabble, draw, sing, drive a racecar, but do things and find out what makes your bell ring. Above all, make sure it's honest, then go for it with all your heart, make plenty of mistakes, learn from every single one of them, and let no one, *NO one*, stand in your way.

On a Lighter Note, Our Tattoos

I HATE TATTOOS. ANYONE WHO knows me will vouch for that because I've always been pretty vocal about it. Natural is best. Pure skin is so beautiful. Why would anyone ruin that perfect design with a permanent picture made of die etched forever under their skin with a very sharp needle?

Me.

Yes. I know I hate them. Most models have them, but they are discreet and in hidden places (which, of course, are limited). So that begs the question, "Why get one, if no one can see it?"

Even though I refer to them as the "tramp stamps," I would and I did—so, never say never.

I blame Joe for my lapse, my indiscretion. We'd been dating a few weeks, and we were in that giddy love and fun stage where you tend to be more daring than usual. Besides, we were both high on love.

So . . . one night we had a lovely dinner at Katana and a few drinks. Afterward, Manny, our limo driver, was cruising around so we could watch the sunset when Joe suddenly said, "I want to get a tattoo."

I was surprised. "What?"

"Simple. I want a tattoo. I'm in the mood. I want to have your name tattooed on my penis."

Now, I was really startled.

"What? You're drunk."

"No, I'm not. I only had two drinks."

"Well, it doesn't matter. I'm not letting you tattoo your thing."

He laughed.

"Joe, think about it. If something goes wrong, you'll be scarred for life. It will hurt like hell, and it might even affect our sex life.

He laughed again.

"Well, okay. But I'm going to get your name tattooed somewhere on my body tonight."

Joe leaned up and told Manny, "Stop at the first tattoo parlor you see."

Not more than a minute went by before Manny pulled over. He remained with the car as Joe tugged at my hand, nearly dragging me into this small, strange tattoo parlor that didn't look very clean. There were two guys working on two customers. Another man in his fifties, with tattoos covering his entire body, greeted us. He was literally a walking billboard for the "art." Though he was a white man, he had long dreadlocks and fingernails to match.

"How can I help you folks?" he asked in a deep raspy voice.

"I want a tattoo, Joe responded. "I want her," he added, pointing at me, "name tattooed on me forever."

The man laughed and said, "Okay. Have you thought about where you want me to put it?"

Joe thought about it, I'm sure thinking he'd tell him his first choice, but he refrained. "Here," he said, pointing at his ring finger.

"Well, let's hope her name isn't too long. What is it?"

"Suelyn," he answered. "All one word: S U E L Y N."

"Sounds Asian," the man said.

He showed Joe where to sit, I followed and said, "Joe, are you sure you want to do this?"

"Yes. Absolutely."

Knowing how determined he is once he gets an idea, I left him alone and began taking pictures with my phone.

After about 20 minutes, Manny entered the parlor to find out what was happening. (He can't sit still very long; so when he's waiting for us, he often wanders and tries to get into other people's business, mainly ours!).

When he approached the artist's area, he looked at the preparations and then said, "Ms. Suelyn, Mr. Joe going to get a tattoo?"

"Yes, Manny, indeed he is."

Meanwhile, the artist spoke up and asked Joe what font and color he'd like.

"I think dark blue. The font, I don't know. Why don't you sketch something for me to consider."

"Okay," the tattoo artist said, taking out a pad and pencil. He wrote *Suelyn* in large script with an even larger capital S, at least as large as what would fit on Joe's finger. I could see it now. It would look like a ring when it was done, a permanent ring. *Aw, how romantic.*

It seemed painful as I watched, but Joe said it didn't hurt. Felt like the guy was rubbing sandpaper on his finger.

Voila! When it was done, it looked like a ring, and it looked *great*!

Okay. A couple of drinks. Joe got his finger tattooed, so I decided that I would, too. Everyone laughed when I said I wanted the same thing.

"You want your name on your finger?" the dreadlocks man asked seriously.

"Noo-uh. I want one on my finger that reads Joseph, J O S E P H," I spelled for him.

"She's just kidding," Joe said. "She hates tattoos."

"No, I'm *not* kidding. Come on, let's do it," I said to dreadlocks.

With Joe and Manny looking on, I jumped into the chair and stuck my hand out. "Make the script blue, just like Joe's," I said.

It didn't hurt and it was over in minutes. Despite the blood and alcohol running down my hand, all was well. Joe looked at it, took my hand and kissed it gently, *"Bellisimo,"* he said, and I could have sworn I saw a tear in his eye.

It wasn't over yet, though. Joe pulled at Manny's shirt. "Come on; you're next, amigo."

"No. It weeel hurt," Manny protested in his strong accent.

"Naw! It won't hurt. Didn't you just watch Suelyn? Are you telling me you are weaker than a woman?" Joe teased, cajoling Manny.

"Well," Manny said, thinking about it. "Okay. No, I am brave. I will put my wife's name on my finger."

"You won't be sorry," Joe said. "She will love you for it. You'll have her in the palm of your hand—or rather on your finger," he said, laughing. "It will make her happy. See how happy Suelyn is?"

With that, Manny sat down and dreadlocks began working again. This time he sketched out the name *Maria*. Then, he began to draw it on Manny's finger with the needle.

"*Ayyeee*," Manny said in a loud voice. "This hurts." And then he squinted through the rest of the short name. When dreadlocks was done, Manny took one look and said, "Berry nice. Berry nice. And at least, if my wife leaves me, there are many, many Marias in Mexico." We all cracked up.

Brazilian Fire Hose with Joe

F ROM THE MINOR TO the movie scene variety, Joe and I have had our share of "incidents" in clubs. I've had drinks intentionally and repeatedly spilled on me from above and had to have security escort people out, because my own egregious behavior.

There was a time in Brazil when Joe and I were returning to our hotel room from a club, and we were being a little too loud. We were standing on a balcony off one of the hallways when a security guard asked us to keep it down because it was late.

Unfortunately, we had been drinking a little too much and after a brief interlude, we got a little loud again at which point the same guard came back, this time looking like he was going to ask us to leave.

I'm not sure what happened to me, probably the alcohol (one of the reasons I rarely drink) but instead of complying and going to our room, I walked right in front of the guard, smashed the fire extinguisher glass, and pulled out the big canvas hose.

Stunned at what I'd done, the guard backed off. He looked at me as if I was holding a gun. Then I did the even more unthinkable—I turned the hose on the guard, and he went flying and tumbling down the hall.

As if I'd been in an out-of-body experience, I immediately came to my senses, asking myself, *How could you do that?*

However, it was too late. The deed was done. To make matters even worse, instead of helping him, our eyes just grew to the size of teacup saucers, as I dropped the hose and Joe and I took off running toward our room. Inside, we pushed the deadbolt closed, put the chain lock across the threshold, and sat on the bed to catch our breath.

Within a few seconds, the guard was outside pounding on the door, demanding to be let in. Sitting quietly, we didn't say a word, holding our collective breath, hoping he'd go away. After a few seconds, the pounding stopped. We started to smile as if it was funny and then realized it wasn't—so we continued to sit quietly until the phone rang, and rang, and rang. We ignored it and eventually went to sleep.

Had we been in the States when this incident took place, things would be different; I would probably have been on another *TMZ* video, but in Brazil, the desk manager simply asked me, "What was going on last night?"

"You mean about the security?" I asked innocently.

"Yes, Ms. Medeiros, and the fire hose."

"Oh, that."

I had to think quickly. Not wanting to go to jail, I said, "He was harassing me so I had to defend myself."

The second I said those words, I wanted to pull them back. I was ashamed of myself, of my behavior. I could stand back and see that I was not taking responsibility for my stupidity or my drinking. *God, I wished I hadn't had so much to drink,* I thought.

There was a long silence and then the desk manager said, "Well, I'm not sure what happened. All I ask is that you replace the fire extinguisher box and pay for any other damages."

"Certainly," I said. When he then began to apologize to me, I felt even worse.

I had seen or experienced so much rude and stupid behavior, usually in clubs, that I was mortified that I was now one of those idiots. I've had men chase me, pull on my hair, and women intentionally spill drinks on me over and over, and I even had to punch one man in the face who was bordering on the violent; but that incident in Brazil was my last night of drinking out.

At the time, I was remorseful because I thought of all the "high and mighty" attitudes I'd displayed myself over people who drink and do drugs. I was always better than that, but apparently not. I'd succumbed to the same lack of judgment that I abhorred. I was not a good role model for any young girls, not even myself.

After that night, I can't say I became a teetotaler, but I never drank that much alcohol again. I've never had a drinking problem and I'm not about to start now. I might have a single drink at a party or during a social situation, but I nurse it all night, never allowing myself to lose control like I did that night in Brazil.

Sometimes you have to see yourself in the mirror clearly and then change your behavior. It could have been worse. Fortunately, it wasn't.

Editorial

People will treat you the way you allow them to . . .

I AM NOT AWARE OF who said those words first, but many people know and say this phrase from time-to-time, primarily because it's true. Now, that doesn't include "everyone" or, obviously, no one would have any friends, ever fall in love, or get married. However, it is one of the sad commentaries about our culture, as well as many others, that *survival is all about the fittest.*

Models are a case in point. Fortunately, we don't all fit the stereotypes. Because of what Hollywood is and does, and how show business (magazines, television, movies, music, fashion modeling, and even sports) treats the people who make it "show business," there are those who want to make as much money and achieve as much fame as they can in the shortest period of time. However, burnout, anxiety, fear, and a host of other emotions begin to take their toll.

Take for instance the paparazzi. Yes, the fans demand what they serve up, and so there is a market for what they do. However, this "profession" has gone way too far. (Apologies to my friend, Brian). You've heard the stories, I'm sure. Celebrities in car accidents, being chased by overzealous photographers, celebrities' children harassed and endangered—just about anything to get that $10,000 to $100,000 killer shot.

Models develop reputations as well. Because of how we are portrayed, people think we are all ding-dongs, fake, arrogant divas. The common thinking by those who don't really think very much, is that the only way a beautiful woman gets to the top, becomes famous, makes a lot of money, or is a celebrity is because she managed to sleep with the "right" man (or men).

Few people who aren't "fans" will give an attractive woman the benefit of the doubt because the jokes always portray models (particularly blondes) as ditzy, dumb, full of sex, and short on brains and common sense; but that isn't always true.

The real story behind the smoke-and-haze curtain that separates "Hollywood" (or celebrities, in general) from the public is that, for the most part, these are real people, in many cases, true artists with talents that most folk only dream of having. But that's okay because a good actor that has found his/her calling is no different than a good electrician who loves what s/he does. And that's the real truth of the matter.

We/I have feelings. I have the same kinds of insecurities that many other people have. I have the same fears, wants, and needs. The women who sleep their way to fame or fortune usually don't get anything even close to what they expected—in fact, they usually just get a bad reputation (and *nothing* kills a career faster than a bad rep, because you can't "un-ring the bell").

I always tell my sisters and cousins, "You are a prize, no better or worse than anyone else. Once you give up the prize (sex, love, reputation), then you no longer have the prize.

No matter what happens, if you don't watch it, all you're left with is your physical looks and then you find yourself being treated the way you allowed someone to treat you. Your self-esteem is so much more important than a quick roller coaster ride. It might be very thrilling, but when it ends, it's all over, and you don't have a damn thing to show for it except maybe a little nausea and a small memory of the "ride" that you'll forget before you get home.

When you believe in yourself, people sense your confidence. They sense a strength that they admire or, in some cases, can be jealous of if that's how they choose to feel. That isn't your decision. Your only decision is to build your confidence, believe in yourself, and always try to do the right thing.

An old friend once told me how to know which of the choices you're confronted with, in just about any situation, is the right one. Sometimes there are numerous shades of gray.

"The right choice," he said, "is almost always the one that is the toughest to make."

I haven't always made the "right choices." No one does. We all make mistakes but, of course, the key is to learn from them and not make the same ones again.

In the business of modeling, movies, music, etc., you can bet in today's Internet-driven world that when you fall, everyone will see it. When you make a mistake, everyone will be there to judge you. Unfortunately, it's not only actually making a mistake, it's when others intentionally lie and make up stories about you to further their own agenda. That really hurts—and there's very little you can do about it.

A few words to the wise: Live your life as if everyone will know everything you are doing (because they will). Always try to do the right thing. Believe in yourself no matter what ANYONE says. No one is your judge and, likewise, you shouldn't be theirs. Make the best of all your talents and know you'll get some lucky breaks every so often to make up for the disappointments. In the end, you'll truly get everything you deserve.

LeBron Tartar

BEFORE I RELATE THIS, I'd like to share the following caveat . . . First, I want to be clear that I am sharing this story, not because I am proud of my actions in any way, but because I believe deep down that I did what I had to do to defend myself.

There are times when we find ourselves in a situation where we feel unsafe, threatened, or disrespected. What should we do? The answer to this question depends upon you and the situation at-hand.

Women, in general, are seen as being weaker and more fragile than men. Unfortunately, some men take full advantage of this cultural bias. I have often seen successful, very powerful men abuse their power. They take advantage of women and get away with it on a daily basis. The examples are endless—and those are just the ones published in the media.

However, there are some stories that leave you wondering which party was at fault. Sometimes it's unclear if a nasty incident involved a man overpowering a female; or a crafty, slick woman took advantage of a situation for money, power, greed—whatever.

A great example of this is the Mike Tyson rape case. Some looked at the story and said, "Tyson—an aggressive Heavyweight Champ, standing at five-eleven, weighing 250 pounds—raped that poor 19-year-old, innocent petite pageant girl."

Others, like me, might look at the story and say, "What is a girl that has no sexual intentions doing with a man in his hotel room at 3:00 a.m. after having gone on a date to which she agreed?"

What was she thinking? Perhaps she thought they were going to play chess or talk politics? I doubt it.

In any event, being a young woman is not easy. I say this from hands—on (no pun intended) experience. I have been in very uncomfortable situations throughout my life, trapped with no options. With time, I learned how to avoid potentially bad situations, all the way from uncomfortable to dangerous.

I have developed an intuition bordering on psychic for male behaviors. In an instant, I can navigate my world and weed out the good from the bad, and the real from the fake. It's like seeing an accident happen on the highway and choosing beforehand to take the side streets to avoid it.

However, even with my uncanny instincts, I still find myself in some very uncomfortable situations, which the story I am about to tell you clearly illustrates.

Sometimes in life we have an option to act and take matters into our own hands in order to defend ourselves from abuse, disrespect, or just plain bad manners. Since this particular story is still so vivid in my mind, I am telling it in the first person.

It is 2009. I am in Paris shooting for the TV Show *Boom Latino*. Tonight is a big event, the premiere of the movie *More Than a Game* starring LeBron James.

I am going to the event with my friend Christen, who is also my assistant. There's a party after the premiere ends. As they say in Paris, a "crème de la crème" party; the best of the best. We attend. Upon arriving, I can see a long red carpet and lots of flashing lights from the press. I do my walk on the carpet, take a few pictures for the press, and then enter the venue. As I look around, I see many familiar faces. Delicious appetizers and drinks are also being served. The best DJ in the world is blasting all the greatest hits. Soon the "star" of the night arrives when LeBron James enters through the giant revolving doors, aglow from the spotlight coming from the DJ booth shining on him and following him to his table. Quite an entrance.

As he walks through the crowd, everyone applauds and shouts his name. "Wow!" I say to Christen. We both begin to laugh. I grab another drink and take a sip as though nothing is happening.

Shortly after LeBron's entrance, my friend Mark comes up to me and says excitedly, "LeBron invited all of us to join him at his table," to which Christen says, "Oh my God! Really? We just *have* to go, Suelyn." I had seen LeBron at a few events before but we were never formally introduced.

As we enter the VIP area, LeBron begins to walk my way. At nearly seven feet, he's the biggest man I've ever seen. Suddenly, I feel like I am in a scene in the movie *Honey, I Shrunk the Kids*. Even though I feel so small next to him, I am not intimidated. Approaching me, he says. "Hey, Suelyn. I'm LeBron. LeBron James. What's up?" Then he looks at his five friends sitting behind him and laughs out loud.

I say, "Ha, ha. Funny. I don't know. You tell me. It looks like you have a better view from way *up* there, right?"

"Ohhhhh! Shit! She's got jokes!" one of his entourage adds.

LeBron says, "Okay, okay. What are you girls drinking? It's time for a refill."

"Champagne," Christen says.

I say, "I'm okay for right now; thank you though."

He disregards my answer and pours two glasses of champagne, then says, "No one says *no* to Dom."

There's a first time for everything, I think to myself.

But he's had a few drinks so he's good and buzzed, and trying to celebrate his big night. I don't want to be rude at his table, so I accept the glass to be polite. Christen and I sit down on a comfortable-looking couch in the corner. One of my favorite things to do at parties is people watch. I just sit, sip on my drink, and watch how people act; it's amazing how silly and stupid some can be, especially when they're drinking and using drugs.

I watch as all the groupies come to the VIP area with absolutely no regard for the security. They are knocking down the ropes, just to get in to meet the "stars."

The party goes on for hours. Although everyone is just starting to arrive, I was ready to go. I don't know how some people party nonstop with no sleep. Maybe it's all the drugs.

(Sidebar: One of the interesting things you see when traveling the world is the different rules and laws of each country. In Europe, people smoke and do drugs everywhere. In a club-scene setting, you see it all around you. Nobody seems to care. They'll pop pills, smoke, and take a sniff right next to you. And if they notice you looking, they'll offer you some with a very big smile on their face. Watching people do drugs upsets me because it brings back too many bad memories from my childhood. I grew up blaming drugs for all the bad things that happened to me. *Drugs made people do bad things*—that was my thought as a child. Later in life I realized that some people are bad regardless of whether they do drugs or not. Drugs just give bad people a high—a boost to do what they already want to do. The more drugs I'm offered, which seems to be endless, the more I want to leave. It all feels very uncomfortable.)

Anyhow, I get up and as I grab my coat and purse, LeBron comes over and asks (in what I figure is his most authoritative voice), "Where do you think you're going, missy?"

"Excuse me; I'm leaving. I hope you enjoy the rest of the party."

He laughs and says, "Um, no you're not. I didn't say you could go anywhere."

Now he's towering over me, blocking my exit and every move! He grabs my arm forcefully, making me go into a seated position as he sits next to me.

"Seriously, Suelyn, why are you leaving so early? I was really planning on getting to know you better tonight."

"You're drunk. Please step back. You're making me feel extremely uncomfortable."

Completely disregarding what I say, he grabs a drink and puts it right in front of my face. "No, I'm not drunk, buuuuuuuuut you need to be! Hahahaha," he laughs.

His friends are close by, laughing and screeching a sound I remember from the dirty hyenas in *The Lion King*. He puts his large, oversized arm around my shoulders. It wraps around me, covering most of my upper body. At this point, I'm in complete shock and disgusted, thinking, *This "superstar" has absolutely no class.*

"Come here, baby," he says.

I say in a strong voice, "Okay. Enough! Get your hands off me! I'm telling you, not asking you! I'm not your baby!"

Since the music is playing very loudly, no one can hear anything that's being said. Still with complete disregard for anything *I* have just said, he presses his arm in, bringing me even closer to him! At this point, I feel beyond disrespected and start to feel seriously trapped and threatened. I glance at the small table beside me, looking for a drink, water, or something liquid to throw on him! But all I see is a small plate with three leftover shrimp, that I didn't finish, and a fork.

Meanwhile, with his other hand, he begins to caress my leg. This is my breaking point. In a split second, without thinking twice, I grab the fork and stab him in his forearm as hard as I can.

"Get your freakin' hands off me," I say. "Do I make myself clear now?"

With the fork still stuck in it, he quickly pulls his arm back. He's not Superman after all. His face shows intense pain and anger. I grab my things and leave, grabbing Christen—who is in shock and total disbelief—along the way. "I'm leaving. Are you coming or staying?"

"I'll come with you," she says, walking quickly to catch up with me.

On the way to the hotel, she asks, "What happened? Why did you stab LeBron with a fork, Suelyn? What did he do to you?"

After I fill her in, she says, "You go, girl!"

Do I believe I did the right thing? The truth is Yes *and* No. I don't advise anyone to stab people, but in my case, I was put in a very uncomfortable position. I was being bullied by a man who is probably accustomed to getting his own way all the time. I felt I had to protect and defend myself; stand up for my rights.

In the U.S., due to strict laws currently in effect, things might have ended very differently. I could have been in serious trouble for my actions. In a complete sober state of mind, I might have reacted a little differently, or maybe not. My advice to all women is: Don't let anyone bully you. If you feel uncomfortable, address the situation and let your wishes be known. Avoid situations your gut tells you are going to be problems. Turn off the freeway before the accident. If you find yourself in a bad situation, get out of it as quickly as you possibly can. If you need to, ask for help. No matter how famous, rich, or powerful someone is, they must understand clearly that *no* means NO!

PROLOGUE

The Me You Can't Google

THEY SAY THAT WHEN you work in Hollywood, your life is an open book. Well, now it is; but these are the true stories, not the made-up ones. I could go on for another 200+ pages, but maybe I'll save that for when I'm older.

I'm sure now that this is published, the interviewers will ask why I wrote it, especially at such a young age. Most people think it's "proper" to wait until you've stockpiled a lifetime's worth of memories, experiences, mistakes, and accomplishments. I think I've done that. In fact, I do it every week because that's how I've chosen to live—one day at a time, with no regrets. Nothing is really going to change. I'll continue to make mistakes, although hopefully fewer and fewer as I grow older and older.

There is a saying: "In youth, we learn. In aging, we understand."

The way I see it, life is always a masterpiece, beginning at the end of the birth canal, all the way until they toss the last shovel of dirt down on us.

To define who I was, I don't see life as an accumulation of pluses and minuses to be added up or subtracted when I'm 85. Rather, I see life as a gorgeous painting in progress, where even the first brush strokes of bright red are a sight to behold. Then, as we grow and learn and become wiser, the artist (me and you and God) fill in the details. As we do, the colors can become more vibrant, more alive, and the picture can begin to convey a message with deep, meaningful, and good emotions.

Regardless of whether that painting is an abstract, or a realistic Norman Rockwell, there is a story, there is emotion, there is life.

More often than not, when I'm being interviewed, I'm asked, "Where do you want to be in five years?"

I always answer, "I don't know. I don't want to plan my life that precisely. I've never been a planner. I've always been a doer. I want to live my life, not plan it out."

To me, life is a chain reaction: What I do today will reflect on who I am tomorrow, and where I'm going. We are all a compilation of our many, many decisions and behaviors. If we strive to "do the right thing," life will work itself out.

That isn't to say I'm devoid of goals. I have dreams like everyone else, but I'm more concerned with today than a thousand tomorrows. I know so many people who are mired in planning. They plan for their retirement and then when they get there, they stand on their front porch, stare out into the past, and say, "Is this all there is? What will I do now?" Personally, I think I'll work until I drop dead. I love the challenge of making a movie, writing about my life, and still writing my most personal thoughts in my quirky code in my journals. I love modeling, traveling, friends, great dinners, and even riding the subway whenever I visit New York.

People tend to dwell in the past. If they aren't looking forward, busy making plans, they are reminiscing about "the good old days," their mistakes and regrets, or what could have been. I tell them all to read Eckhart Tolle. End of story.

Here's the deal, one of the most important things I've learned: No matter how much we plan, do the right things, help others, follow our dreams, paint our paintings, and make our movies, there is *always* going to be a setback or two. Even if you're starring in and directing your own movie—even if you have the loftiest of intentions—there will be challenges and people who will envy your success or just plain don't like to see other people be happy. Evil exists. There will always be bad days, even truly horrific ones. But know this: Everyone on earth has gone through the same things. You are *not* alone, and you *will* prevail. You *will* succeed *if* that's what you want to do.

Another question I'm often asked is, "What advice would you give to young girls thinking about modeling or acting?"

I think I've answered that in this book, or at least I tried to do so. However, I will add this: No one will ever live the exact same life as you are. As I've already said: You are the writer, the artist, and the director of your own movie.

I look at my movie as being filmed, all in one take, no do-overs. You truly can make your movie whatever you want it to be. It can be triumphant or scary, as you wish. It's *your* decision. It may not seem like it when you're embroiled in problems and challenges, especially when you're young and it seems everyone else is controlling you, but it truly IS *your* movie.

My early philosophy was "fake it until you make it." If I want something badly enough, I still use that way of thinking. I let *nothing* stand in my way—not the institutions, men, the power brokers, world events—nothing. To paraphrase an old saying: "If I can see it, I can do it." It's really that simple. If you can see your own movie, then certainly it's possible. I don't believe that God gives us creativity, the power to dream, the power to change and, especially, the power to love, only to see us fail and/or live unhappy lives.

When you get right down to it, at its core, life is pretty basic. You only have to control *you*. Take care of your own thoughts, behaviors, and beliefs. You can share them all, or you can keep them to yourself. But YOU are the only one you need to control. There's a way to do that—to change your desire to change someone else—and that's to *LET GO*. Let go of controlling thoughts and behaviors. Every time you let go, you gain peace and energy. If someone says to you, "You're a failure or you made me angry," those ideas aren't yours. They belong to the one who thought of them. It's someone else's opinion. Certainly, we're all entitled to them; just remember you weren't the author. Your peace resides in knowing you are living, as you want to live, and that you are doing the right things in life. You can't control what other people think, which is a good thing for two reasons: (1) You don't want to waste the energy conducting someone else's life, and (2) you don't need to hear what anyone else's agenda is for yours.

You gain peace because you aren't stewing about someone else's conduct. You know who you are and what you want. You gain energy, because you save the energy that would have been devoted to changing someone else; thus keeping it for yourself instead.

I look at the energy that we are all given every day in terms of calories, because that's something most girls think about at one time or another. It's a simple way to decide what I want to spend my day doing.

When I'm about to be in a confrontation, whether it's at the grocery store or on a film set, I stop and ask myself, "Is this worth the calories?" In other words, would I rather fight a losing battle by trying to change someone's way of thinking, or would I rather save the calories for myself to spend in far better ways later in the day (like snuggling with Joe and sharing the events of our day).

Since I'm in show business, I'm sometimes "held up" as an example, which can be good or bad. Most of you have seen the bad ones on the Internet, *TMZ*, or wherever. The public doesn't see what I want young girls to learn and avoid.

I hope when young women read about some of my mistakes, they learn from them and take them with a grain of salt because fame, money, Hollywood, and all the rest of it are oftentimes just a movie created by moviemakers (like the media). Just as you can make your own movie, so can they. So much of it is untrue. But, here's the rub: Much of it is also true. The sadness, despair, failures, drugs, and ruined families should be lessons you don't have to live to learn.

Your duty in life is to inspire yourself with your own dreams and passions, and to always do the right thing.

If you inspire others along a similar path, so much the better. I simply tell all the young girls I meet: Don't do drugs. Don't get caught up in the phoniness of fame and money; they truly do not provide you with peace of mind and happiness. It is only in your own honest and passionate endeavors, and trying to "do the right thing" in every circumstance, that you can find peace.

I once asked a wise old woman: "How will I know what the 'right thing' is? There are so many gray areas in so many decisions."

Her response was: "When you are confronted with a decision between one thing and another, stop and think about it. Which of the two is going to be the most difficult for you? Given our propensities as human beings, more often than not, that is the choice you should make."

The beginning . . .